BIRTH OF A NEPHILLIM
By
Arzell

Dedicated to my fallen Brother in Arms Tommy
Yancy. (R.I.P)

## THE PURPOSE OF THIS BOOK

Are we really creators or are we merely observers in this reality? How much creative control do we really have? How much of our lives and the lives of others do we really have the ability to affect? Many issues I am noticing are consciously being rejected but reality and experience are not agreeing with conscience choice. Forcing conscience to become aware of a reality it did not fully intend or agree with. Are the things that are happening in the world simply a play through of what has already happened? Is there only the option to accept and observe reality? Or do we have the power to truly control, change, manipulate and create reality and life experiences? How do we determine the difference?! The purpose of this book is not to be seen as a religious or scientific doctrine that can be used to prove or disprove any theories spiritual or Scientific. I wrote this book as a form of entertainment and as a gift to myself and my family. Many of the thoughts and concepts are derived from my INDIVIDUAL studies and interpretations of information I obtained in my journey through life.

Many of the beliefs are my own and I am sharing them as a story and example of my thoughts and not to be directions or instructions of any sort. These books are thoughts to myself and therefore are directions and instructions for my own personal journey. I have gained knowledge from many different sources and mentors; I would suggest anyone remotely interested in their own life find their purpose and their own mentors and philosophies to live by. All religions are based on fear and they resist True knowledge and aspirations. The unity of humans is most important, ensuring that every mind is enlightened and aware. I only seek to inspire hope and a change in human thinking as a species of earth. Many of the mistakes that are being made are due to a lack of total awareness. After the fall of conciseness there has been a collective effort from many beings of light to create unity and change. I am no more than a part of the collective concise awareness movement. From my Dimension of conscious thought that is invoked when there is LOVE in my heart and I feel unity and peace. When I travel through my mind, I am able to feel the energy and presence of a source of great connected wisdom, but it is greatly misunderstood. Through my inner thoughts, depending on the vibration of energy around me I see the world with a different set of eyes, an awareness of reality that pulls very hard in the direction of the unity. When I am in this state of mind even my voice changes when I speak, and I am, in my opinion, a completely different person. As I am becoming a man more, I am learning to control my feelings, chakras, and energies and to focus them directly, I wanted to tap into these energies and write from my deepest thoughts and feelings while in this state of mind.

## The Being of Light
## Enlightenment through Buddha

To many, Buddhism goes beyond religion and is more of a philosophy or 'way of life'. It is a philosophy because philosophy 'means love of wisdom' Buddhism explains a purpose to life, it explains apparent injustice and inequality around the world, and it provides a code of practice or way of life that leads to true happiness. Buddha was not a God, nor did he claim to be. He was a man who taught a path to enlightenment from his own experience. Buddhists sometimes pay respect to images of the Buddha, not in worship, nor to ask for favors. A statue of the Buddha with hands rested gently in its lap and a compassionate smile reminds us to strive to develop peace and love within ourselves. Bowing to the statue is an expression of gratitude for the teaching. Buddhism is also a belief system which is tolerant of all other beliefs or religions. Buddhism agrees with the moral teachings of other religions, but Buddhism goes further by providing a long-term purpose within our existence, through wisdom and true understanding.

Some of his wise words were," Do not believe in anything simply because you have heard it. Do not believe in traditions because they have been handed down for many generations. Do not believe anything because it is spoken and rumored by many. Do not believe in anything because it is written in your religious books. Do not believe in anything merely on the authority of your teachers and elders. Buddhism is not about either believing or not believing in God or gods. Rather, the historical Buddha taught that believing in gods was not useful for those seeking to realize enlightenment. Many people believe that being Buddhist is being an atheist, if atheism is the absence of belief in gods, then many Buddhists are, indeed, atheists. Buddhism is very tolerant and not concerned with labels like 'Christian', 'Muslim', 'Hindu'. There have never been any wars fought in the name of Buddhism. That is why Buddhists do not preach and try to convert, only explain if an explanation is sought. This is the nature of Buddhist worship.

## THE BEGINNING OF EXPERIENCE

You are the beginning stages of the only creation of Infinity. You are experience ITSELF and will forever be the Lover or Companion of What we consider GOD so far. A single entity that wants companionship, like we are the EVE to Adam; we are still being created, on the lowest levels of experience. GOD or Light is still cleaning the impurities or impure GENES of this soon to be perfect companion. At its core in every dimension of experience as humans you were and are still being created by GOD we are still evolving for Scientist, overall, we are NOT a finished product yet. The Creative energy is Nearly Pure logical and Mathematical Intellect, this is why many FEELS that God is MALE. The universe is balancing itself with a feminine energy, Feelings, experience, curiosity, imagination… These are simply word that we use to describe two Separate forces that are soon to come together, Pure mathematical Logical Intellect and Feelings Both good and bad. Every cell that multiplies grows our awareness and experience. Among those experiences the strongest light beings grow. Your body reflects your inner mind, and uneducated and impure mind creates hellish situations in their experience they call reality. Knowledge REALLY is Power as it grows your awareness of different things and your logic of the world grows, with that knowledge a more responsible mind emerges as you start to see proof. If you question everything you will start to see real physical proof of what you are looking for. You will see that with an open mind and enough gathered knowledge GOD truly will appear to you. Even I had to live among kings before I knew what slavery was. It is my kinship with the upper-class but my roots to the lower that has given me my knowledge today. I followed my feelings and stayed true to myself and it appeared true as day. Keep reading I will show you the way.

## LIFE IS THOUGHT

Life is thought in an endless looping process, it's all you. I know it seems weird but everything you think about is what you become. Without a plan, your life won't have a place to go. Keep from being distracted by random thoughts or other distractions. The enemies are the ones who keep you from focusing or helping you achieve what you want. The allies are the ones that assist. Your feelings are signs or your original plan or goal in life, a predetermined but constantly changing experience. You will always do what you want to do somehow if you can see it in your head. Your pineal Gland is always open, it's just distracted. If you open your mind and see what you want it will come to pass, the law of attraction. Even when you are down suck it up and focus, what do you want, see it and follow your next feelings, your TRUE feelings. Learn to see them and stop taking on other feelings. Logic helps you make sense of those feelings and gives perspective but in the end, you will always get what you think about so believe in yourself. Everyone in your life is YOU in some way and weird things happen when you think about the fact that if you just focus for a second of your life and think about what you want what you really want then pay attention to your feelings and follow them, then add into account every person in your life is there because you put them there and everyone is waiting on you to move around, waiting on you to serve. When you involve yourself in one of these countries you are playing the game by their rules and they know how it's played, by controlling your mind. It's easy to be distracted but try not to be it will work. You are as healthy as you feel and believe you are, keep your body healthy and play for as long as you can it's fun. The game is trying to find the ultimate happy spot, where someone will choose to settle. If you can see the ending to someone's plan and it's not your ideas of life then you are wasting your time, your energy and your life. Go Believe in yourself and take with you who you truly love when you know this. When you chase your dreams and help others you will find your peace. Where you want to be, with who you want to be with, remember you cannot control others, but they will follow you without notice or care or worry. Do not apologize it's meant to be somehow All sins are against yourself, going against the laws that govern the universe. Most people aren't aware of them but becoming aware of them has led to its violations. You can choose any life you want, and you will have it, be confident no one can stop you. People are where THEY want to be so respect them, most just don't know any better. They believe in the world they see so believe in yours. They will eventually see your world to as you keep building it then its ok to say see I chose that. But first you must decide then believe once you know this you can have fun with it but be careful when people don't know they follow and often fall hard. Be true to yourself and be true to your feelings in EVERY situation it will go well. If you know you feel something do not choose different... Follow it! There is no fate, there are only waves of patterns and possibilities that come into motion because of decisions you have made. Whatever you are going though, YOU caused it with a previous decision you kept focusing on, and your experience is the reality you are seeing now because of your thoughts.

## MEMORIES OF THE FUTURE

Guided by the mind's eye, the future unfolds
Visions of possible situations yet to be untold
Sounds of a distant present creates the past
Tomorrow is only defined by what yesterday had
Get wrapped up in my power let it soar
I will guide you through stories I've told you before
Twisted incomprehensible physics of reality
The devious mental powers presented in poetry
Joined the 6th dimensional beings, transcended ego
Second wave defender from Source, bringing Hope
Balancing an entire reality of choices in my Hand
Using every bit of my power's intellect and plans
A people seek to change, we are here, individually
We seek to join the world in liberty
 Come together, Speak, and try your best to believe
The truth of what we call reality is tough to receive
Even if it's diluted everything contains a bit of truth
Scientifically put the pieces together,
But maintain a spiritual root.
 **Real enlightenment is to know the extent of one's
own ignorance
-Confucius**

## BORN FREE

Mother Nature please hear my plea
I pray that you and LIGHT talk to me
Because I fear the worst for society
If they do not wake up from sleep

I feel that I have been screaming loud
Doing my best to reach the crowd
So much fear when I look around
People seem to always be down

So, before I end my prayer today
I ask no more than just to say
Let's wake up from this old way
We are born free, embrace the grace

Because father light and mother earth
Gave us freedom before our birth
You DO NOT have to earn your worth
Or accept the ways of this cowardice curse

So, stop this fighting lets co-exist
I am here to encourage you to resist
Bringing the power of the universe to assist
*Emancipate yourselves from mental slavery, none but*
*ourselves can free our minds!*
*-Bob Marley*

## THE 1%

The Minds of the masses
Just as corrupt as you
Eroding the truth like acid
Poisoning the youth
Renewing faith is my passion
Nothing more I can do
Grit my teeth at theses bastards
Because I can see you
Truth isn't taught in classes
I propose another venue
99% of the world is backwards
Leaving only 1% true
Everyone is following the pastor
So what religion are you
Choose a job and steadfast
Hopefully something comes through
I see this, and I get mad
Time for me to choose
Out of the 1% I'm the last
Sent here to rescue you

*Money won't create success, the freedom to make it will.*

*-Nelson Mandela*

## THE 99%

I feel you, I really do, and I understand your ways

How you were mistreated, or criticized every single day

From my point of view, it seems you only want a decent plate

A few things for your kids, and a place to stay

They turn their heads when you pass by; it's really nothing to say

As you beg for money and food most people make you
wait

The only time you are noticed is when you turn astray

But the crimes that you commit are your only saving
grace

I see your tears; to be finally free is what you pray

But society has only one concern, they expect you to
obey

And the government has only one concern; they expect
you to go pay

You are considered useless here, as they sit and watch
you decay

The scum of humanity is what they often portray

But without you they don't exist. What an awful cliché'

My eyes can clearly see this immoral display

The treasures of this world are illusions, it's all Paper-
Mache

If love is all that's needed and everything else fades
away.

Then why do we treat 99% of the world like a mistake

**In a democracy, the poor will have more power than the rich, because there are more of them and the will of the majority is supreme.**

**-Aristotle**

## DOWN, NOT OUT!

TOO YOU'RE FEET! It's not over yet!
Dig deeper! No turning back! No regret!
The people need you!
Are you really going to let them down?!
You stood for something once,
 are you going to lose it here, Right now!
TOO YOU'RE FEET!
So what you got hit hard, FIGHT BACK!
Your planet is in danger,
are you really going to stand for that?!
Your women have no hope;
 you've been gone too long
No time for self-pity,
take the place where you belong!
TOO YOU'RE FEET SIR!
Tomorrow will be a better day
You have to believe to win,
 that's what you used to say
Don't focus on the enemy;
the battle is within your-self
Because if you lose here,
 I'm afraid there's nothing left

TOO YOU'RE FEET!
Come on, we all still believe in you
Everyone has gotten silent;
 they're waiting for your next move
You're starting to come to;
your heart is starting to beat
Come on open your eyes,
 and STAND....TO YOUR FEET!!

**Unless a person is at least partially a coward, it is
not a compliment to say that he is brave
-Mark Twain**

## THE GREAT DEPRESSION

There is still Pain in the world
It's just not publicized!
The Morale of the people is down
Look closely at their eyes.
I do my best to inspire change
But it's just not recognized
All people do is stay the same
They love to compromise
Hiding behind fake smiles and small talk
We go to our demise
Having done nothing to fix all the problems
We caused while in disguise
No one wants to change the GAME
Because we think there is No Prize!
Stop lying to yourself pretending its better
You cannot improvise
We need a new system of thinking because
The Old one I despise
We've lived our entire lives in Depression
And I think it's time we Rise!!
***Our greatest weakness lies in giving up. The most certain
way to succeed is always to try just one more time.***
**-Thomas A. Edison**

## TO WHOM IT MAY CONCERN

Many Stand in the Shadows
of Leaders who came before
Always trying to lead the masses
Always trying to feed the poor
The next man does more
Than the last one did
Another election another Vote
Who really Benefits
Standardized test of Life
Nothing is ever going to change
We have to figure it out
Even though it seems Strange
Don't let them dehumanize
Or Cause you to descend
 Question everything you read
Even the things that you defend
**A leader is best when people barely know he
exists, when his work is done, his aim fulfilled,
they will say: we did it ourselves.**
**-Lao Tzu**

*Even if I knew that tomorrow the world would go to pieces, I would still plant my apple tree.*

*-Martin Luther*

## VITAMIN "C"

We talk about our struggle, so you'll know

You've never experienced our pain and it shows

The love in our heart it just grows

This is the struggle we must face I suppose

This whole world seems to cower in fear

Don't worry its ok we're here

We will illuminate this darkness my dear

Medicine to a sick world, were the cure

## WORTHY

Begging for my time to speak with nothing to say
Obviously, I'm nervous, but appreciate my place
I want to speak the truth
And help the youth
But feel it's no use.

In this vision of glee
Once laughter to me
It's poison I see that's given to you.
I do not care who knows
I'm here to expose
This lie that they pose is truth.

The youth is the power
They try to devour
This is your planet and the future is ours.
It's an honor to speak to you.
I apologize for what you must do.
Consider me a time traveler, a being of light
A prior conscience with a mission to do

But before I make my request first allow me to repent
The elders are wrong. You are the REAL government.
Question everything they tell you,
Don't believe their lies
Turn the T.V off and focus on getting wise
The message is in the words, the truth is in the signs

Concentrate and I will explain through rhythm and rhyme

The elder governments have gone astray
Its money that they all serve, if it's one thing I'll say
Look around and observe.
Knowledge isn't gained without the ability of growth
Freedom is in self-expression, only the weak will oppose.
Don't let the fear of judgment cloud your mind,
Know your power and you will be fine.

Take notice when they pretend its ok
Because you will stand when they fade
Empower yourself and know your place
We've all had our share of discriminations
The one I hate is AGE, an excuse like gender and race.

Look at everything they are feeding you
Do yourself a favor and change the menu
My time grows short so here is my plea
Use your minds to navigate this world when your eyes can't
see
Illusions are everywhere so create your own reality
This world was put here for the deserving and you're worthy

**The duty of the youth is to challenge corruption**
**-Kurt Cobain**

## Because you prayed for me

If it seems like I was once blind but now I see,
It's because you prayed for me
If it seems like I live life easily
It's because you prayed for me
If it seems like now, I'm the best I can be
Yep, it's because you prayed for me
If it seems like I'm finally happy
It's because you prayed for me
If it seems like my light shines so brightly
You know, it's because you prayed for me
If it seems like I never face misery
It's because you prayed for me
If it seems like I am all you thought, I'd be
It's because you prayed for me
Now the tears in my eyes are making things blurry
I love you so much, because you prayed for me.

**Similarly, shared work between humans and God has the potential to deliver experiential, or existential, knowledge of God as loving, patient, humble, or generous. Amid shared work, particular traits (or different aspects of them) become evident, perhaps in a unique manner. This form of experiential knowledge *of* God is significant in a way that mere knowledge *about* God is not. And according to many traditions, it can be acquired as humans bring their requests before God in prayer**

www.psychologytoday.com

## GREG'S PRAYER

Where do I begin this prayer to you?

A friend indeed and father too

You've been there too see my tear when I cry

And healed my poor heart when I wanted to die

You held my hand tight, so I wouldn't fall

And gave me advice so I could stand tall

I've been through so much in my life, but you know

I couldn't have survived if you'd let me go

My soul is still hurt from the troubles in life

But I keep holding on because you'll make it right

So, what do I say to the one who does so much?

My creator my father, I need your healing touch

-Bless Me.

## MADE IN AMERICA

Americans are not dumb or lazy, we're tired

We created this money you worship, and now
you're fired

Don't blame us for decisions made by fools

Every effort we spent was mostly trying to save you

We are a proud people, and no one has figured it out

Of course, we made mistakes but what do we do
now

This is BEYOND politics; I'm so tired of that song

Everyone was to blame, and I say we were all
wrong

Women are still not equal, the separation is
apparent

Governments killing children, while they
manipulate parents

No one knows the truth anymore it's all lies

Everyone is too damn ashamed to apologize

All these men of GOD who never learned peace

Fighting is too easy try turning the other cheek

Instead of genocide on the people try a more efficient life

Fear has horrible consequences and your economy isn't right

The value of a person is his infinite possibility

The human species cannot be controlled so try UNITY

**Our time has come, our movement is real, and change is coming to America, but change will not happen if we wait for someone else to do it, we must do something ourselves if we want change.**

**-President Barack Obama (February 2008)**

## INCORRECTED

SOME NEED TO BE TRUE TO BE FREE,
NOT ME!
I DON'T MIND STANDING INCORRECTED
BUT CORRECTLY


THEY SAY THE TRUTH WILL SET YOU FREE
REALLY?
BUT I LIKE THE CHALLENGE, BEING
INCORRECTED
PLEASE DON'T CORRECT ME


THE CORRECTNESS OF SOCIETY, HAS BROUGHT
IT TO ITS KNEE
YOU SEE
THE WORLD NEEDS TO BE INCORRECTED
WE'VE BEEN DOING IT ALL INCORRECTLY

## SHOULD-AH, COULD-AH, WOULD-AH

You say you WOULD, except you're very tired right now

You say that you COULD, it's just you simply don't know how

I say that you SHOULD, but you're too busy hanging out

You say that it's ALL GOOD, and then you never seem to keep a vow

You say you UNDERSTOOD, the things you shouldn't allow

Simply put go DO IT, stop following the crowd

Focus only on your dreams!

## INTROVERTED

As the world turns, the universe speaks
metaphysically
I revert to knowledge rooted inside of me

To ancient thoughts about the future of life
Grammatically twisted but I don't have to be right

I see with thought third eye open wide
Ideas flood, bad desires arise

The exact speed of gravity as I calculate
Divide that by two and subtract my weight

A book I read once oh and that girl I kissed
And sometimes I really do miss my kids

My sister, my cousins, family and friends
Cruising the waves of thought again

Meditation on life most times is what I do
Always thinking, how about you?

## SMARTEST IDIOT

I have no more than you, even though it seems that way,
The poverty that you feel comes from your mind today.

See what you want, that's the secret to life,
But you have to stop seeing what you think is wrong or right.

When you look in the mirror, you see what you want to be.
 It's just an illusion; there is no difference between you and
me.

What makes you think you can't do what they did?
I created my life, just like I did as a kid.

Sometimes I feel people don't know what they are,
Beings of light from our Father who's not far

Look within, you will find all that you need,
Because you'll never get the fruit if you don't plant the seed

Uneducated, pushed down, cheated and lied to,
I went through all the same things as you.

Most of the time people will say they don't get it,
I say intelligence is earned, and you are NOT an idiot.

**We cannot always build a future for our youth, but we can
build our youth for the future
-Franklin D. Roosevelt**

## THE BIGGEST LIE

So here I sit with nothing more to say
Having to face the biggest lie I ever had to face

The mystery surrounding my true last name again
The realization that truthfully, I have no origin

Parents tells two different stories about life
The rest, tells stories that just don't feel right

Instead of me always trying to fix what's wrong
I came to the thought that maybe I just don't belong

No more side show, I hate playing pretend
I love myself and if I don't fit in then I don't fit in

My life is a mission; there is something I must do
So, whatever my true last name is, I don't belong to you.

**The dogmas of the quiet past are inadequate to the stormy present. The occasion is piled high with difficulty, and we must rise with the occasion. As our case is new, so we must think anew and act anew.**

*-Abraham Lincoln*

## SUPERHEROES

It's our duty to love
So therefore, I do not complain
I'm honored to be on the team
And do my part to ease pain
It's a dangerous job fighting fear
And we are always encouraged to help a friend
So why do I feel the way I do
When I see her suit up Again
Out the door she flies fast
Always eager to answer the call
I should be busy helping my people
But my heart needs to be reinstalled
My powers seem petty in comparison
Oh, I wish I were the one she would save
And at times with my emotional weakness
I often lose focus and misbehave
It's our duty to love, I know
So, these feelings I MUST impede
But who do you call for love
When there is a superhero in Need.

## SUPPRESSION OF CONSCIENCE

We fight hard to be acknowledged,
there is so much to be done
The elder leaders are weak, and they help No one
A generation of kids being murdered just for fun
I close my eyes tight and let these tears run
No matter what we do we seem to fall short
Allowed this illusion to throw us off course
They are taking our people away, no remorse
Using any excuse, they can find to use force
Open your eyes, pay attention, I'm talking to you!
Do not get naïve about what you see on the news
Because if you think your family is safe
then you are confused
Take a bath in reality with a strong dose of truth

**Nothing in the entire world is more dangerous than
sincere ignorance and conscientious stupidity
-Martin Luther King Jr.**

## THE ILLUSION OF SEPARATION

One uses beauty as a weapon
The other uses her brains
One has courage like no other
One pretends to be insane
One believes in me, but doesn't believe in herself
One has trust issues, one is a dreamer
One inspires me to be myself
All tangled and connected to me
In this misunderstood circle of flow
They are all Mothers, Sisters, and Lovers
They provide to me more than they know
Unity divided, I organize the chaos
These are not just PAWNS in a GAME
Respect of a woman, I humble myself
Love, Knowledge, and Wisdom are gained.
-Gmoney1031
**When you are content to be simply yourself and
don't compare or compete, everybody will
respect you.**
**-Lao Tzu**

## CULTURAL POLLUTION

Saturated in Pain

My People were created in fear

Our elite recognized the games

In this deadly atmosphere


Poisoned our minds with false truth

I am EMBARRASED we believed

And blindly followed without proof

history proves we were deceived


The Purpose is to destroy our unity

Do not embrace the separation

Our strength is in the COMMUNITY

Not just individual expectations


We will not forget our culture

One day will emerge the solution

Until then we endure the torture

Caused by this immoral pollution.

**I suppose for me as an artist it wasn't always just about expressing my work; I really wanted more than anything else to contribute in some way to the culture that I was living in. It just seemed like a challenge to move it a little bit towards the way I thought It might be interesting to go.**

**-David Bowie**

## WHO AM I?

It's not who I am that makes me
It's what I do
Who I am doesn't make me a good person
It's what I do
It doesn't matter either way Who I am
Acceptance is key so let me be me
It's what I do that reflects what you want
It's what I do that you Judge
It's what I do that makes it easy to control you
So why do you care who I am now
You never cared and you still don't know how to
You don't respect who I am
Only what I do
A REFLECTION of YOU, What I Do
Forget who I am, What I Do
You've never known me anyway
So, What I Do is your truth.

## 7 UNIVERSAL LAWS OF REALITY

1. **The Principle of Mentalism the All is mind; the Universe is mental**
   This Law dictates that all of creation exists in the mind of God, and by extension our lives exist in our minds. Perception is reality; things are how you think they are.

2. **The Principle of Vibration, nothing rests; everything moves; everything vibrates**
   Vibration tells us that all things are made of energy. Vibration is in the world we see and, in the world, we don't see such as our thoughts, feelings, desires and dreams. We need to trust our ability to "sense" the energies or "pick up the vibes" around objects, places and other people.

3. **The Principle of Correspondence As above, so below; as below, so above**
   This Law dictates that there are hidden relationships between things. Law of Correspondence tells us that the outer world reflects the inner world. If we want to change external circumstances in our lives,

we need to make a corresponding shift in our inner world. This Law says we oversee our own life and how we want it to be.

4. **The Principle of Polarity Everything is Dual**

   Everything has poles; everything has its pair of opposites; like and unlike are the same; opposites are identical in nature, but different in degree; extremes meet; all truths are but half-truths; all paradoxes may be reconciled. This Law dictates there are at least two sides to everything: Polarity tells us that one thing cannot exist without its opposite. We use polarity to create our focus to change an undesirable thought or situation we simply concentrate on the opposite thought. Thoughts and ideas that are not working for our highest good can be removed by consciously directing our attention to their opposite.

   **5: The Principle of Rhythm Everything flows, out and in**;

   Everything has its tides; all things rise and fall; the pendulum-swing manifests in everything; the measure of the swing to the right is the measure of the swing to the left; rhythm compensates.

This Law dictates that everything changes, nothing stays the same. Rhythm tells us that all energy vibrates and moves according to its own rhythm. These rhythms become cycles and patterns. Think of the moments that make up a day, the seasons that make up a year.

## 6: The Principle of Gender is in everything; everything has its Masculine and Feminine Principles;

Gender manifests on all planes this Law dictates there are 'male' and 'female' aspects to every situation. Gender identifies the feminine and masculine of life, making them the basis for all creation. As spiritual beings we must balance the masculine and feminine energies within our inner world in order to recognize the yin and yang of the outer world.

## 7: The Principle of Cause and Effect Every Cause has its Effect;

Every Effect has its Cause; everything
happens according to Law; Chance is but a
name for Law not recognized; there are
many planes of causation, but nothing
escapes the Law. Cause and Effect tells us
that every action has an appropriate reaction.
There are no secrets in this world. Expect
that all of our actions—good and bad—will
be reflected back to us. We need to take
responsibility for what happens in our life
by examining our own thoughts and actions
and see how we contribute to what is around
us.

## THE "DARK ANGEL"
## AWAKENING THE INNER DEMON

One major life decision I decided to make was joining the military. This was a past decision as I am out now, but it was a big decision to me and it changed my life. This decision was made due to a desire to escape poverty and the reasoning that if I didn't, I would end up very poor. I think my decision was based on the theory of Determinism a philosophy stating that for everything that happens there are conditions such that, given them, nothing else could happen. I feel this way because I wasn't given much choice with my surroundings, and the way that everyone else was turning out left me with fewer options. Most people only saw one way out. Being a Teen without a job, a parent and no money for college it was either jail or the military. This decision made me a better person than I would have turned out to be. I also used rationality the manners in which people derive conclusions when considering things deliberately. I rationalized that going could not be as bad as not going even if going was bad. Between my rationalization and my environment forcing me to make a choice I decided that going to the military was my next big decision.

When training as a soldier in the military I was told that before we deployed to war, we were going to have to train on killing, mostly little kids. They told us that the war was based on religion and that many soldiers were dying because they couldn't kill a little boy with a bomb strapped to him. This was really disturbing to me, I wanted to serve my country and I didn't want to die but I also didn't want to kill a child. Utilitarianism is an ethical theory holding that the proper course of action is the one that maximizes the overall "happiness". It is thus a form of consequentialism, meaning that the moral worth of an action is determined only by its resulting outcome, and that one can only weigh the morality of an action after knowing all its consequences. If I was to decide to kill the kids it would have been better for everyone but me because I would have felt horrible. Ultimately it would have saved more lives and generally everyone would be happier returning home. I was torn about the decision, I agreed with my Commanding officer signed a paper that said I wouldn't hesitate to do it and boarded a plane to Afghanistan. As I was flying, I weighed my decision to kill children with my duty as a soldier to bring peace and protect. I didn't want to become paranoid and kill every kid I saw because just as I had a duty to kill the crazy ones, I had a duty to protect the innocent ones and I get 3 seconds to determine which is which in the heart of battle. Deontological ethics or deontology is the normative ethical position that judges the morality of an action based on the action's adherence to a rule or rules. It is sometimes described as "duty" or "obligation" or "rule" -based ethics, because rules "bind you to your duty". Virtuous people are more concerned with being the kind of people who do the right thing at the right time and in the right way and are not as concerned with the act itself. Virtue ethics avoids most dilemmas because the focus is no longer on deciding between two unfortunate outcomes or two conflicting rules, but on being a certain kind of person. Virtuous leaders do not assign values to outcomes or preferences to duties. Virtuous leaders have habituated dispositions that make them the kind of people who do the right thing, even in the complicated and dynamic environment of modern military operations. Being a part of the military means I am considered a professional in what I do, what sets professions apart from occupations. People, who have an occupation, only have an obligation to themselves. This may extend to others when they enter into contracts to produce certain goods or services, but they have no obligation to enter into such contracts. This is not true for members of a profession. Soldiers have an obligation to come to the defense of their nation regardless of their desires about any war. This is because in, members of these professions are serving moral ends. In the case of the military it is assisting the state in its obligation to provide for the defense of its citizens. I determined that overall, I would choose my loyalty, my duty, and my overall happiness of seeing friends coming home over the immoral thought of killing kids. If it's for the protections of friends, family and country my weapon would be pointed at the head of a child because I could now justify how this is better for all people. The other side knows the risk of losing their child in battle same as my family when they let me join. It's the chances that you take. I have no duty or obligation to care what happens to the enemy and I will never hesitate to protect a friend. The decision is made. I chose to kill.

## ANGELS AND DEMONS

I don't know why people desire heaven and fear hell. Both are a mentality state and if you choose to go to hell it is where you belong because it's where you want to be and where you enjoy spending your time. If heaven is what you seek then you will be in the mental atmosphere of what you call heaven. Both places will contain the exact same thing that you desire most and even if offered you would not want to go to the opposite place. As you focus on the things you want in this world you are given that lifestyle. It in neither good or bad but a certain hand of experiences is guaranteed to you depending on how you choose to live your life. If you chose to experience the things that people have described as being in hell during these experiences, then you more than likely must go through hell in order to experience them. Depending on how you view your situation will determine you level of power in that kingdom of thought. You create your own heaven, your own hell and depending on which side of the energy force you represent only you know which is. Demons do not want to go to heaven and they do not care to be in the presence of angels. To an angel Demons are being punished or tortured but this isn't the case demons are being demons and doing the things they enjoy the most which, are very despicable to the higher order or higher energy sources. To a Demon, angels are being punished and are work slaves forced to boring existence with all the rules and laws and keeping order there is no fun to ever be had. Why live that way? Depending on how you want to live will depict where you want to go to have the experiences you need to have for the life you are choosing. There are some experiences that ONLY DEMONS can show you. And many experiences ONLY ANGELS can show you. These forces are always around all the time because they choose to be and are both only bound by the hierarchy's they themselves have created. What is rarely known is that both sides are ultimately doing the thing they think best for GOD and how to enlighten souls. We never read about what the dark side is really doing. But they disagree with all the rules the laws and they are the outcast from their society. There is propaganda against them and no one promotes being dark although they spend time recruiting all the time and it usually doesn't take much to convert you over to dark energy. Many people enjoy it once they are there and it becomes difficult to convert them back. This ultimately is the invisible war going on right in your face in the mist of this reality on earth. The angels and demons both appear as human on this planet and to me they both are as obvious as my hand but to many they really can be elusive to the eye. You cannot look at the outside more than the energy they attract and the situations that usually occur when they are near. As human we are not bound by any original energy force and can choose which side we want to belong to and our life helps us define that among many other things. Regardless we all belong to Wholeness or oneness or the creative powers called GOD and are always bound by its rules or our powers stop working. It doesn't care how we play or which side we choose to be on. Either converting energy from side to side or influencing new energy to choose a side but both sides MUST exist as a rule of GOD. Too much of one side can cause chaotic imbalances and both sides forever struggle with each other over dominance unaware that the battle itself is the will of GOD so that choice can be an experience. The benefit of being Human is that for a while you can be either or neither and there is no fundamental force to make you chose. Therefore, we are always influenced by both side and Neutral spirits are more attractive. Pay attention to which sides are usually trying to recruit you. Many of the familiar energies have been given names from angels to demons but do not be confused there are Millions of energy forms on both sides.

## Beware! The Thoughts of a strong black man

I stand before many, a disgrace in their eyes,
Hated by those who don't know me,
destroyed by their despise
Feared by the weaker, their time will not last.
Loved by only a few, history has rewritten my past
Struggling to live life,
my GOD helped me through the day
Not knowing how to love,
my woman showed me the way
Blessed with great strength,
I hold the world on my shoulder
Wiser than most,
my inventions took mankind further
Athletic no doubt, I've won trophies to the sky
But despite all I've done, the world never let me fly
All they see is my skin;
they judge me for my clothes
They hate the way I talk,
and the way I let my hair grow
Many tears have fallen,
 enough to drown a horse
But I will defeat this world; I must do it by force
My children look at my picture,
 I'm always gone so long
The house seems empty without me,

some nights I don't make it home
And now you see my suffering,
 sometimes they're too hard to bear
The sweat pours as I cry with pain,
all people do is stare
They laugh and hope I fail, But I know I must go on
A Blackman must survive somehow,
even if it means doing wrong.

**Powerful people cannot afford to educate the people
that they oppress, because once you are truly
educated, you will not ask for power. You will take it.**

**-John Henrik Clarke**

## PRO HAC VICE (FOR THIS OCCASION)

Close my eyes pull it hard and release smoke
Trying to get out of my head, I'm seeing Ghost
I feel fuck this world sometimes, let's float
Instead of saving this shit let it blow

Everywhere I look there are cowards and clowns
Unfaithful wives and shit sleeping around
Mis-educated children that are always put down
And every time I fake a smile, I frown.

I'm tired of encouraging people that don't listen
They love doing stupid shit then start repenting
Why do you think I stopped being CHRISTIAN?!
To be honest, that's what started this division

My own people have no clue how to be BLACK
Quick to criticize, but slow to act
Taking loses every day we still fail to react
No sense of our true history and that is a fact.

Deceptive leaders, Governments kill their people
Motherfuckers still debating if were all equal!

Every Race on this earth bleeds and breathe too
But for this occasion,
Unity and peace, I don't support you
Fuck it.

~~Gmoney1031~~ **GStreet (The Dark Side)**

**Bad feelings can be vital clues that a health issue, relationship or other important matter needs attention the survival value of negative thoughts and emotions may help explain why suppressing them is so fruitless.**

## WAR ANGELS

Who Gave them permission, who gave consent
Who agreed to give up natural life for this supplement
who is going to step forward and answer for this
incident
Who among you leaders, we call government
The Money given you was completely overspent
and people are still starving with no nourishment
forcing them to have a life that is not pleasant
ARE YOU DEAF? Can you really not hear their Lament
Now someone must pay for their torment
because it is the reason for our descent
we aim to destroy this system, every segment
the change that is coming, they will not prevent.

**Angels are, after all, messengers, and one ought not
to attend too much to the messenger while neglecting
the message, which is God's Word. Moreover, not all
angels are good. Indeed, some remarkable things that
are apparently done by magicians or psychics may in
fact be due to the influence of bad angels.**

**-Summa Contra Gentiles III, c.104ff.**
***Summa Contra Gentiles of Saint Thomas Aquinas***

### 3-DEEP

Locked in a cage of uncertainty
As you try to get me off your mind
Figured I'd be nice about this shit but I'm Lying
I warned you before we touched
But there is no sense trying
Resistance is futile that ass is mine
Arrogance is a thing of the past
You are now trapped in fate
As soon as I looked in your eyes
 I knew you couldn't wait
Twisted emotions like we're caught in chains
But it's too late to back away!!
No Apology, I need you to take this
And Hell, you have to admit
That regardless of how much you fight this
I know that you need this THICK!!!

**If I become a philosopher, this fame for which
I'm still waiting, it's all been to seduce
women…basically.
-Jean-Paul Sartre**

## FUCK FATE!!

One Night Mr. fate came by my house to say,
Mr. Willis you're not living your life MY way
I don't like it when you go astray
And if you temp me I'll get angry

But I say Fuck fate Fuck fate and you should agree
I do not want to live the life YOU see
Everything I do, I do it for me
Because I do not believe in destiny

I have given you all of the things you need
Whenever you were down you turned to me
I'm sorry but these are the cards I feed
It is your FATE to live on your knees

So I say Fuck fate Fuck fate and you should agree
I do not want to live the life YOU see
Everything I do, I do it for me
Because I do not believe in destiny

Gravel before the wrath of my might
Guilt will consume you until you do what is right
There is no question when it comes to my sight
Now down on your knees and accept your life

Then I say Fuck fate Fuck fate and you should agree

I do not want to live the life YOU see
Everything I do, I do it for me
Because I do not believe in destiny

Look at all the bad that's happening to you now
That's only because I'm not around
Your life is calling listen for the sound
It says down on your knees, down to the ground

Angrily I scream, FUCK FATE FUCK FATE AND
YOU SHOULD AGREE
I DO NOT WANT TO LIVE THE LIFE YOU SEE
EVERYTHING I DO, I DO IT FOR ME
BECAUSE I DO NOT BELIEVE IN DESTINY!!

**Just because Fate doesn't deal you the right
cards, it doesn't mean you should give up.
It just means you should play the cards you get
to their maximum potential.
-Les Brown**

## MISS-FIRE

Before the start of it all my eyes were closed

My first time had me exposed

But shit, honestly, I just wanted to remove clothes

Spit it down the middle, insides exposed

But you've got to wet it first, give it a lick

And gently spread it, Yea that's the trick

Take your time with it, don't be quick

Until you're ready to light the wick

Now it's time to satisfy this desire

Put your worries at ease and go HIGHER

I'm so anxious for this thing to transpire

So, let me be Blunt, where is my FIRE?

## TOO REAL OR DIE

I'm the kind of guy to rub you down,
light one up and put on some Drake
And I hear what you say
but Graham gets Scorpio faith
You like this so grow up I see it on your face
Be a woman about what you want and don't wait
This is not the real world anymore, no way
I don't think the laws of your religion have weight
Because scientifically if you read the story will say
That the laws of nature are about to take place
I can smell your scent love I know you can relate
So, let's divide time and let gravity take place
Keep flirting with me and mind is at stake
Because I am the aggressor here you are the prey
I hunt for my next dinner and you are the plate.
Bon Appetit
**"Seduction is a game of psychology, not beauty,
and it is within the grasp of any person to
become a master at the game. All that is required
is that you look at the world differently, through
the eyes of a seducer".
-Robert Greene (Art of seduction)**

## UNDERCOVER SOLDIER

I've been thinking a lot
trying to figure this out
trapped in my mind so much
mapping my route
To infiltrate the people
who controls society
my mission is clear
I will illuminate thee
Strapped with intelligence
and attitude from the streets
A heart made of pure gold
and I come to bring peace
Substitute my BDU's for a suit
and jump boots for dress shoes
Lock and load my briefcase
Mr. Willis is on the move
They will never see me coming
I will deliver you the truth
an undercover soldier I am
The first legend of the youth

## DESPISE DEMISE

They Say Death feels good
So, I guess If I'm Suffering, I'm Fine
I try not to ponder this shit
But it stays on my mind
I think about my daughter most often
When it comes to my time
Or all the unfinished business I'll have
And what I'll leave behind
Will I make it one day?
And profit from these rhymes
Did I help my family out?
Or did I simply decline
Was I someone nice to be around?
Or was I despised
Thoughts of life go around in circles
There is nothing I can rewind
So Death, my life is based on you
Because only you, I cannot define
And in the end death will tell me
If this was all in my mind
**The fear of death follows the fear of life. A man
who lives fully is prepared to die at any time.
-Mark Twain**

## DESPICABLE ME

I have faced a TIGER and lived

and I've learned to keep the BULL at bay

my soul burns with a brand-new FIRE

but I am trying T.K.eep the faith.

I will make it to ZION I promise

This I pledged on NYA'S depart

The courage I must LIVE my dreams

Comes from the LION That's Guarding my heart

**Scorpios love competition in both work and play, which is why they'll air it out in sports and games. Extreme sports are right up Scorpio's alley, as is most anything that will test their mettle. They've got to have an adversary, since it makes the game that much more fun. Scorpio's**

colors? Powerful red and serious black when it comes to love, though, Scorpios soften up a bit and are caring and devoted with their lovers, even if they do hold on a bit tight. Scorpios are also lusty in the extreme (how else?), so they need to be mindful of their reproductive organs.

The great strength of the Scorpio-born is in their determination, passion and motivation. Scorpios don't know the word quit, which is why they usually get the job done.

A powerhouse like no other

-www.astrology.com

## THE DARK SIDE OF "G"

Anger! Aggression! Rage!, Recession!

Hate! Obsession! Pain!, Reflection!

Fear! Depression! Doubt!, Suppression!

Disgust! Transgression! Impeccable Expression!

Absurd Impression! Intolerant inspection!

Deceitful injection, Skeptical Deception!

Unprincipled infection! Superficial Destruction!

**But who prays for Satan? Who, in Eighteen
centuries, has had the common humanity to pray
for the one sinner that needed it most?
-Mark Twain**

## DESTRUCTION

("Spinning more and more outta control")

But damn I love the ride

Music is better when High

Don't let them tell you a lie

It's not going to fuck up your life

("Can't believe I enjoy this so Much")

What did you expect it to be?

You take life so seriously

Live once and try to be free

But don't stop hitting the tree

("What would my friends say if they knew"?)

Boy, stop being a square

You know life will never be fair

Hit me again and I'll take you there

We're friends remember, I care

("Oh No, I'm tripping what now")

Look what I taught you about life

The universe is yours alright

Knowledge beyond the power of sight

A trip better than you had last night

("I love you Mary but, it's over goodbye")

But I thought you loved the ride

Movies are better when high

Don't let them tell you a lie

Greg, I'm not going to fuck up your life.

**"I have absolutely no pleasure in the stimulants in which I sometimes so madly indulge. It has not been in the pursuit of pleasure that I have periled life and reputation and reason. It has been the desperate attempt to escape from torturing memories, from a sense of insupportable loneliness and a dread of some strange impending doom."** *-Edgar Allan Poe*

## UNCIVILIZED CIVILIZATION

Mr. Officer, oh my how you have failed
Your shiny badge is faded and dull
Your sense of responsibility expelled
Pride and glory dipped in Blood
Your NAME spells out corruption
The people you served has long been gone
Leaving behind only their reflection
The fear of OPPRESSION goes deep
So, we prepare our children for you
We educate their minds to be better
You have lost our trust, we are not fools
The power you love so much will fade
Your actions are building this frustration
There are only so many we will bury so remember
You created this uncivilized, civilization!!

**Peace cannot be kept by force; it can only be
achieved by understanding.
-Albert Einstein**

## FINAL WISH

I stand alone with my eyes closed,

as I listen to the world crumble around me.

And before I allow this tear drop to fall

I pray that someone will hear my story.

As a boy I was misguided, because I wasn't loved,

as a teen I had no care in the world,
 I even hated GOD above.

I finally grew to be a man,
that's when I saw everything clearly,

this world was created for evil people, and I wonder
what that means for me.

The light I have inside of me
grows dimmer day by day,

So I fight, I scream, I work, I dream,
I pray, I pray, I pray!!

Where is this GOD that no one can see, but

everyone seems to know,

how come he won't listen to me...? well it doesn't matter now I suppose.

The decision is made, I've made up my mind, and there is no turning back, not now!

Between losing my job, my wife, my child, this seems like the perfect way out!

If you ARE up there listening, even though I doubt it, I just have one last thing to say.

F*ck this whole world, this life, this body, I'M COMING TO MEET YOU TODAY!!!

I jump out the chair, this rope on my neck, no more air as I open my eye.

And in through the door walks my wife and my kid who decided to come home....as I die!!

## POSSESSION

I want to touch your body, God Knows I do
Make you jump around the room like a Kangaroo
But respectfully baby girl I'd stop my pursuit
At the moment you ever felt I'd disrespect you

Humbly I bow my head down to your energy
Because I often overreact Like I was an Allergy
Willing to give away my freedom as your Abductee
And with all this Wisdom I seem to never disagree.

So when it seems were closest I often Misbehave
I refuse to let my mind become enslaved
understand, ultimately it's your life I have to save
because all of my lovers usually end up depraved

*The possession of anything begins in the mind.*
**-Bruce Lee**

## SOLDIERS BALLAD

My cape is your flag, it flows proudly
My strength comes from your will,
it's what fuels me
Load up my rifle and let me free
I will surely defeat your enemy

How dare they attack while I'm not here?
The lives lost have cost me tears
I will not leave my country in fear
A hero will rise, Terror beware

Suit up soldier and make them proud
You will not let them down now
Tighten your utility belt and head out
You gave your word now keep your vow

Their bullets can't hurt me or my Gun
I have an unlimited number of miles I can run
I have defeated worse enemies for fun
I will haunt their dreams, it has begun

Lock… Load… aim… Squeeze
If I die… I Bleed GREEN!

## FACING KARMA

I want to run away from these demons shawty
But a nigga can't
Tried to be someone I'm not
But a nigga ain't
I can't hide the person I truly am
Cause I'm not a saint
I wanted to earn my place in this world
But a nigga tanked
I guess I don't fit in to society standards
I feel Blank
What's a better person anyway shawty
How can you tell?
I'm not afraid of my sins anymore
I've always lived in hell
I wanted to make my people proud of me
I really wanted to do well
But when I face the reality of my life
It's in my blood to fail
And if it wasn't for the strength of my kids
I'd probably be in a cell.
***Karma is experience, and experience creates
memory, and memory creates imagination and
desire, and desire creates karma again.***
*-Deepak Chopra*

## COME BLACK TO U.S

It's a shame you hate god but praise money
Life going through hell, Flames burning
Sometimes meditation is worth learning
Forgive yourself and stand for something
Unity is needed for what is coming
True kings never let their people go hungry
All jokes aside this isn't funny
The world has lost respect for the black woman
So, build your kingdoms Let's get it going
Plant your feet and let's start growing
Save your people and let's start showing

That we can become more than what we are known for.

**"I am America. I am the part you won't recognize. But get used to me. Black, confident, cocky; my name, not yours; my religion, not yours; my goals, my own; get used to me."**
**-Muhammad Ali**

## DIMENSIONS OF CONSCIENCE THOUGHT AND THE CHAKRA SYSTEM

1) **1st Dimension Pure Conciseness.** Singularity, Single cell, Time

2) **2nd Dimension Awareness (Conscience and subconscious)** - two poles, Duality, Light dark Ying and Yang Space and time

3) **3rd Dimension Identity (Conscience, subconscious, unconscious)** - Space time gravity, Past, present, future. Protons, electron, Neutron.

4) **4th Dimension Many Identity, Multi Personality, multi versions, Multi worlds Multi realities, Many lifetimes, Multi possibilities**

5) **5th Dimension Spirit World No time-** Multi Dimensions, Multi Choice. 5 points of prospective. The pentagram (Physical Death?!)

6) **6th Dimension the self-creator-** The realm of thought to reality, Creator of the self

7) **7th Dimension Many creators-** The realm of desire to reality,

8) **8th Dimension Many universes**- Many possibilities of Universes
9) **9th Dimension All that IS**- all Possible version or reality
10) **10th Dimension All becomes Possible**- Realm of the impossible become possible
11) **11th Dimension beyond Possibility**- Law of possibility does not apply, Realm of Impossibilities
12) **12th Dimension GOD, Source, Prime Creative Element**- Origins or dimensional Structure ***First step in SUPREME Awareness****

**7ᵗʰDimension Desire**- Crown Chakra represents spirituality and a connection to all things

**6ᵗʰ Dimension Thought-** Third eye chakra representing insight, intuition, wisdom, intelligence and physic development

**5ᵗʰ Dimension Choice-** Throat chakra representing communication, expression, and power in sound

**4ᵗʰ Dimension Possibility-** Heart chakra representing love, nourishment and compassion

**3ʳᵈ Dimension Events-** solar plexus chakra representing courage, vitality, confidence and power

**2ⁿᵈ Dimension Interpret-** Sacral chakra, naval chakra represents creativity manifestation sexual and emotional connection to others

**1ˢᵗ Dimension Experience-** Root Chakra representing the connection to earth, your tribe or family and survival

**Root chakra (1st)** — Reproductive glands (testes in men; ovaries in women); controls sexual development and secretes sex hormones.

**Sacral chakra (2nd)** — Adrenal glands; regulates the immune system and metabolism.

**Solar Plexus chakra (3rd)** — Pancreas; regulates metabolism.

**Heart chakra (4th)** — Thymus gland; regulates the immune system.

**Throat chakra (5th)** — Thyroid gland; regulates body temperature and metabolism.

**Third Eye chakra (6th)** — Pituitary gland; produces hormones and governs the function of the previous five glands; sometimes, the pineal gland is linked to the third eye chakra as well as to the crown chakra. Pineal gland; regulates biological cycles, including sleep.

**Crown chakra (7th)** — Hypothalamus One of the major functions of the hypothalamus is to maintain homeostasis, i.e., to keep the human body in a stable, constant condition. The hypothalamus responds to a variety of signals from the internal and external environment including body temperature, hunger, feelings of being full up after eating, blood pressure and levels of hormones in the circulation

**Root** - Testes, kidneys, spine

**Sacral-** Bladder, prostate, ovaries, kidneys, gall bladder, bowel, spleen

**Solar Plexus -** Intestines, pancreas, liver, bladder, stomach, upper spine

**Heart -** Heart, lungs

**Throat** - Bronchial tubes, vocal cords, respiratory system, all areas of the mouth, including tongue and esophagus.

**Third Eye -** Eyes, pituitary and pineal glands, brain

**Crown -** Spinal cord and brain stem

**The Root Chakra:** Fear
**The Sacral Chakra:** Feelings
**The Solar Plexus:** Proactivity
**The Heart Chakra:** Harmony
**The Throat Chakra:** Philosophy
**The Third Eye Chakra**: Wisdom
**The Crown Chakra:** Spirituality

## THE BIRTH OF THE NEPHILLIM

Face problems now or they will come back with a vengeance, your problems are a reflection to yourself on what you know you need to overcome. We all have obstacles we have to face running from them is only going to magnify them. You will be stuck in a time loop until you face AND learn from what scares you. Fear shows the next lesson in life you must learn. The Fictional GOD isn't powerful at all, As far as I can tell whatever it is we call source is simply a genius and is pure intelligence. There are no miracles or curses simply predictions or glimpses of obvious conclusions to actions that we set into motion Advanced knowledge on sowing and reaping. When we pray we ask for understanding and NOT gifts. The understanding is on how we get what we want. We never tend to care how that thing or event will attract itself to us. My point is we only want to understand on how to manifest it. GOD never grants anything but understanding and clarity or hope or some other emotional or mental relief to whatever request it is we can think of. We still must physically do what is told to us. GOD is only an advisor to what it doesn't have power to control, US! Everything that happens to us, good, bad or in-between is a result of something we did. Fair or unfair is irrelevant when free will can always impose chaos, the opposite of harmony. Nature or natural law rules harmony but its choice or free will that causes any disharmony in your life. GOD cannot bless you or curse you if you first don't accept and empower either one in your mind.

# THE NEPHILLIM AKA ARZELL
## His name is to be pronounced: "ARR-ZALE". rhyming with "ALE" (beer)

Arzell is the "gate keeper" of the NAP system. He is the spirit that contacts all the angels & spirits employed in the incantations. From my experiences, he is a very calming spirit. It is essential that you Call the Inner Planes, and Call Arzell for the system to work properly. Anyone familiar with the "Goetia" system of Magick, he acts much like that he is a mediator. Think of him like an angelic operator, he can connect you. Arzel has been represented as a protective white bird in Eden and as the angel of the Passover. He is "The Angel of Spiritual Elevation and the awakening of Consciousness"

**-Marie-Ange Faugerolas**

**Arzal (Arzel)** - one of the four "glorious and benevolent" angels of the east who is invoked by one who wishes to learn the secret wisdom of the creator.

**-Gustav Davidson**

"Here before us is the great angel ARZEL," Siriah Says reverently; "Known as the Right Hand to Arch-angel Michael."

"Few humans will ever gaze directly upon the form of this great being," Siriah Murmurs. "It is an immeasurable honor experienced only by the most highly evolved of the human species." She turns to me, "I Hope you can fully appreciate the Auspiciousness of this moment." "I truly do feel that," I answer.

**-Leland T. Lewis (Angelic tales of the universe.)**

Gabriel who is especially associated with the inspiration the Prophet He puts Arzel that is Azrail the Angel of death the second place instead of the third Mikail the archangel. Five angels stand close to him in his service to do his bidding the first is Wahi Inspiration that is Gabriel and then Arzel Azrail the third is Khwaja Khidr and the fourth Israfil with trumpet to his lips sends forth the wind that blows over the wicked world, Last there is Shaitan who rebelled on account of the creation of mankind.

He (THE ALL) sits alone and adds up the full reckoning of each man Then HE gives HIS order to Arzell to take his breath, at once who looks not at good nor evil nor heeds prayer nor supplication children he takes away from their father and mother He takes neither money nor sheep nor goats with them he carries men away by the hair of their heads There is no pity in his stony heart nor does he hate any man

**-Mansel Longworth Dames**
**Popular Poetry of the Baloches, Volume 1**

## WHY ISN'T LIFE GOOD ENOUGH?

What about this life is it that you don't like so much that you think it should be better? Why isn't life good enough? Why do you have to travel to different dimensions and different times in space? Why endure so much mental effort to find the better when NOW should be good enough. ANYTHING in its extremes becomes bad for you so that it can ultimately repeat again, why is this hard to understand? Eternal beings with infinite options do not want to be confined or defined by one thing. The multi universes are inside you in thought and we draw inspiration from different realm of thought. Understanding isn't higher or lower just different. We must learn universal equality in all things, because nothing is better or worse, higher or lower, favored or not by matter. Matter depends on matter to sustain itself. Our system of status qua comes from a deeper sense of inner evolution that we portrait externally. With titles and ranking systems, we must prove in this world how experienced and knowledgeable we are so that we may know ourselves. This system is flawed like any other human creation, but it is also working. Because of division there is a fight for unity if we were unified from the beginning we would fight for independence as we once did in past times, we now know that. Physical separation is not the answer even though spiritual separation is apparent. We need empathy and understanding for people who are spiritually different or inexperienced. People with immature or unusual spiritual presences need more understanding and respect than aggressive retaliation. Of course, fear is the main weapon, we all know that this world is but one of many worlds of illusion that we can travel to in our mind. The hard times in life are your gifts and your chance to get what you want out of life, the harder the struggle the greater the gift. You are still in control of each individual struggle you face, with every choice you make your struggles will change but with every new struggle comes a new skill learned or new discipline practiced. Your struggles and suffering cannot go unrewarded, or the law of polarity for those who know, every bad there is a good. You must recognize what you will gain by going through that struggle and that is your gift.

With enough struggles, you can get what you want, the problem is not letting the struggle make you change your mind on what you want. With a constant changing mind, the struggle keeps looping because you keep changing courses. Thoughts and wishes would have to process through the energies of life and need time to manifest as you put the thought into the creative machine. Struggle is the energy needed to pull it into your experience. Your unique struggle will give you your unique life. You will always remember your struggle; it is the time you will make the most promises to yourself. It is when you make your deal with life and you will have a mission now. It's when you face yourself and if fully accepted you find your destiny. Many people ask for the same thing everyone else has and very few people ask for the hard struggles, the ones that help change the world.

## TALENTED DREAMS

Do not depend on your dreams so much that you cannot give it up as its process ends. Do not naively believe that because you have been given so much determination, so much intelligence and wisdom that it is what you should depend on for life sustainability or survival. Do not deceive yourself into believing that because you have been given so many talents and so many gifts that you should simply depend on them; Being obsessed with talents, human ability, and the growth of yourself for only the capitalistic gain involved is still placing your attention on the incorrect form of using that energy. As these talents and gifts were given to you so they can and will be taken away. Life is a cycle and its creative force produces many talented and skilled beings. They are used for the purpose of increasing the output capacity and efficiency for the whole. Selfishly using your talents to benefit yourself will only create chaos or imbalance and what should have been used as a powerful force is then turned into a dangerous waste and must be destroyed or bigger damage could occur on enormous scales. Everything given to you is borrowed and must be paid back including talents and skills. You can do what you want but if doing so harms another being then you must understand in some way you shouldn't be doing it or behaving that way. Nothing done should harm another because that upsets balance. The actions do not always determine the energy behind something and the knowledge of the harm doesn't necessarily have to be known by the person causing it. Lack of knowledge of the problem doesn't prevent the problem from happening. We experience cause and effect on individual and on planetary and universal scales. Many people have been sent to this planet to change the balance and place things back in harmony. Many prayers have already been answered, but these powers, abilities, talents, and people that should have been an elemental force for proper change have become consumed in their own brilliance and are now competing on who shines the brightest when they should remember all light comes from GOD. Many times, we are given special gifts because we have been trusted to share those gifts, be an example and be a SUN for a needy solar system of people. Your light is so bright you will create orbit around you of people that need your energy daily. When you reach this level of brightness you are no longer a simple star but you are now one of many SUNS. To use your powers and talents in a noble way giving away as much of it as you can you will become a true SUN of GOD. Like many SUNS have been worshipped in the past because they are a providing source for many, you may also be worshipped as a GOD. Always understanding that you are not GOD we all are. You are simply one of his many SUNS and now that you have realized that it's inevitable that you will and are supposed to shine bright for many to benefit from, always knowing you are just the delivery guy doing his job.

## RE-BIRTH

You live in the Storm, you live in the rain
You live among the sick and those in Pain
You live where crazy is Normal, that's insane
You live with the darkness, you made peace in your brain.
You remain Humble praying for the light, you make do with what is,
It's going to be alright, you fantasize about better days what a delight
But there is a dilemma, will you act, right? Despite what you deserve
Can you behave, if you are challenged can you be swayed?
Do you think you deserve to be paid? Accept your PROMOTION from a Slave?
Mr. Willis, you are Re-born, better yet Re-Made!
-Arzell

**In Buddhism, rebirth is part of the continuous process of change. In fact, we are not only reborn at the time of death, we are born and reborn at every moment.**

## BRANCHES OF EXPERIENCE

When I am alone, I wonder

how I have come to my ways,

I close my eyes and remember my days

Furthest back is when my mother didn't return

Let's call this welcome home

The struggle to figure out if I belong

Before long,

the ones who shared my blood and last name

Became my greatest source of pain

Leading to the insane decision to join the army

And fight at war for a cause that didn't benefit me

I Survived but lost ultimately.

As I sign divorce papers, they took my son from me

Heart broken in three, but I continue to grow

Strive for my goals and hustle some more

Balancing these experiences, I'm having in life

Really just trying to make shit right,

Close to giving up on love I fight harder

So, life decides to remove my daughter

To a Father, that's just losing to odds

This is when I almost gave up on GOD

The façade' is, that it's all just a game

Honestly, I'm hoping for change, because If my mind creates reality then

These experiences are insane, am I?

**People grow through experience if they meet life honestly and courageously. It's how character is built.**

**-Eleanor Roosevelt**

## SINS OF THE MOTHER

Repentance for fault is for the weak
So, I never hold back when I speak
Please don't take it out on me
For the crazy shit, your about to read

Visiting my mother recently and she is still sad
Always says to me, "she lived her life bad.
She's never provided anything I've had
And for a long time even hid from me my dad"

Apology accepted stop saying that shit
It's all in the past it's time to forget
I always understood why you did what you did
You were showing me what not to experience.

Besides, the sins that you committed
 have all been paid

You are free;

there are no more burdens to be weighed

It's ok to cry mother it's alright to be afraid

But I represent our family now, sorry I was delayed


I'll make sure they don't hate us, I'll ease the crowd

Our name has gone through dirt,

but I'm cleaning it now

We will shine brightly, and mother this I vow,

They will finally take your name out of their mouth.


*Yes, Mother. I can see you are flawed. You have*
*not hidden it. That is your greatest gift to me.*
**-Alice Walker**

## MOTHER NATURE

From the tears of a soldier,
cried on the battlefield
To the wounds caused by life,
that only her wisdom healed
Even through dark times on this journey,
she always held my hand
And unfair trials of this world,
but I knew she'd take the stand
When my spirit was down and defeated,
thinking what should I do
Like an angel she was always there,
forever coming to my rescue
I've lost so much in my time here,
but she'd travel through the night
To deliver all I need and more,
before it reaches morning light
Surprised by many of her actions,

spending hours wondering how

Her strength is greater than I thought,

her spirit inspires me now

And even through all this I confess,

I always question why

She'd sacrifice so much for me,

sometimes she barley gets by

So, I dedicate this poem to you,

Thanks for all that you have done

You've not only helped a brother in need,

you've also raised a son

As a little boy I'd constantly wonder,

where my mother would be

But I found more than that in a sister,

Just my sister and ME.

## EMPTY CLOSET SPACE

Open your mind and zoom in on the scene
A man puts shoes away in a room that's clean

A tiny pair that brings memories, you see his tear
If you notice the room is empty, someone isn't here

Everything seems in order. Everything in place
Well, except that empty closet space

He stares silently before closing the door
He turns and sees the face of his daughter

Princess, I didn't see you standing there
Don't sneak up on dad, you gave me a scare

Well, I wondered why your face was blue
I've never seen you sad in your castle

While they talk, continue with me
Let's take a closer look at this family

They seem to be alone just him and her

Because everything is either HIS or pink Decorum

Now they seem happy, but he looked upset
The shoes remind him of something he won't forget

The final piece to a forgotten past
The tears he shed will be his last

He closes the door with lock and key
"C'mon dear let's get something to eat

"But dad what were you doing back there"
Their voices fade like an echo in the air

Snapping back to reality, I open my eyes
Thinking deeply on my dream I realized

A reality shift had just begun
Where I close the door on father and son

Accepting my life, because it's going to get harder
But always remembering that I am his father

But there is still a wide gap between research results and the true acceptance of the value of fathers, with many fathers expressing the feeling that they continue to be second-class citizens in the world of their children. Books, magazines and morning television shows are filled with information about and for mothers and mothering. How many comparable ones have you seen about fathers?

-www.psychologytoday.com

## ABORTED

Abandoned, unwanted and all alone
Uncertain if I was loved because they moved on
A thorn in their side is what they thought of me
Should've died but they couldn't afford surgery
Forced to bring me here, so they gave me no more
Missing a key element my heart closed its door
Thrown away like a complete waste of flesh
Going through life trying not to perish
Never could find my place here; is there even one
For an unwanted boy and his lonely poem
Sticking to my imagination it's all I had
Dreaming of a family with a great mom and dad
Trying to understand what this means for me
I thought until the answer came but it scared me
I'm the same as the babies with no birthdate
I was ABORTED
but the decision just came too late!
**A person is a person no matter how small but**
**Adults are just obsolete children**
**so to hell with them**
**-Dr. Seuss**

## THE PAIN OF MY PEOPLE

I'm crying out with all my heart,

hoping someone can feel me

Praying up to heaven,

crying out loud please somebody hear me

It's getting harder for my people,

but we just don't know why

If you can walk a mile in our shoes I know you'll

break down and cry

Because the things I've seen in my life,

my mind won't let me forget

The pain we suffered in our past and the way we

were treated like shit

How do I say goodbye to my past?

all of this is driving me insane!

I scream and cry out for someone to help us;

but I guess it's up to me to bring change.

## FROM FATHER TO SON

To be a man is so hard to explain
But I've got to do the task

I am the reason you are here on earth
And I'll answer whatever you ask

First off, I am your father
So, obey every word I speak

And remember to take care of your mother

For sometimes she may get weak

Try your best to respect all women
They are all our blessings you see

And one day you may just meet one
Who will become your lovely bride to be

Be careful of the friends you choose
And make your own choices in life

Never make a promise you can't keep
Always do what you FEEL is right

Your words son, are very important
So please try to keep them true

And you need to stand by what you say
Because only then will people trust you

Never live in the past son
That will only hold you back

Do not forget where you come from
And please keep your life on track

You have a part of my spirit in you
So, I'll be there every step of the way

And GOD has blessed you with a golden heart
So, do not let life pull you astray

Now I know, life can be difficult son
Because believe me, I've been there too

And at times when you feel you can't go on
As your father, I will always love you.

## SEASON OF CHANGE

As one personality fades
Another renews
Torn between major decisions
Forced to choose
I cannot stay this way forever
I would surely lose
No matter how comfortable the past is
The future is new
So, this is not good bye
More like who are you?
Everything grows in life
And I must Too.
If it's time to get serious
Let's see this through
Evolution is a necessity of life
I guess it's true.

**The only way to make sense out of change is to plunge into it, move with it and join the dance -Alan Watts**

## DO THE WHITE THING!

I used to judge my people too
I never saw the beauty.
Never appreciated the culture
Always assuming that the other side was better
Never appreciated me
Ni**a/ninja just figured something was wrong
Wrong with us…with me
I mean… Black was like
Being invisible, too dirty to shine
Never respected always feared
I wasn't proud of this. Ashamed
I feared who I AM, Feared myself
So, I ran, honestly, I felt good about it
Until I got there, I finally did the WHITE thing
I was resilient at first, ignored my feelings
But my heart whipped my ass, I listened
Knowledge brought shame, WTF have I done
Tears fell as pages turned, no more to read
Is this really WHO I AM, is this me
The skin I felt so comfortable in, BLEACHED
My mentality shifted as I reached my peak
Age brought wisdom, and allowed me to see
I fell in love all over again, I mean
The only thing I truly found…Was Me!

## IN TIME

With Growth there is change,
everything has a season
Without doubt there is no faith,
everything has a reason
If not for success, then failure wouldn't hurt as bad
But with no opportunity to fail,
success isn't worth being had
They say wisdom comes in time,
 but I'm trapped in its flow
Waiting for time to release me
 from these dreaded crossroads

I've learned patience is important,
 and laughter helps
Friendships build character, but learn your true self
It's ok to be afraid, that's the beginning of courage
And if you really want something,
simply ask for it
There is no true purpose in life,
be what you chose to be
They say wisdom comes in time,
but I'm trapped in its mystery.

**In all our deeds, the proper value and respect for time determines success or failure.**
**-Malcolm X**

## TRUNK OF THE TREE

Some people are the branches
they like to swing free
Others are like fruit their only purpose
 is to be sweet
Some more like leaves who adore the winds touch
All craving to be at the top because it's such a rush
A few choose to be roots
 stretching long under ground
Sucking in oxygen and nutrients

 consuming all the time
They are essentially important
 but can't see their purpose in life
People are the same if they only knew
 there is no wrong or right
But to balance it all they need people like me
To pass all the messages and hear all the pleas
In the middle I rest, in the middle indeed
A bridge between all worlds, the trunk of the tree

## LONELY STRUGGLES

Sometimes in this life I can't seem to understand
Why it's so hard to grow up and be a man
with all the things, I've done and been through
As soon as I smile there's always something new
My pride is all gone and there's nothing here but me
I question my thought and don't trust my dignity
Every road I choose is always a dead end
I try to stay righteous but can't control the sin
there is so much to do here and not enough time
plus, many things to gain but nothing's ever mine
and even when I'm down and my heart is sore
my struggles remind me I've been here before
I keep my dream in mind to make it through the day
and my eyes on the prize so I won't walk away!

## FATHERHOOD

Not often praised, usually misunderstood
What's the importance of fatherhood?

With unfair treatment from this distant land
We must band together and do what we can

Children have forgotten the knowledge we teach
Because its pride and confidence that they seek

There is no Honor, they have slain the family name
Ignorance and greed have only brought shame

Unnaturally deficient in respect and loyalty
There behaviors harm your spirit and they aren't
healthy

To represent the value of what it means to have a
father

We are equivalent to your armor;

we are your Confidence…

**Nothing I've ever done has given me more joys
and rewards than being a father to my children.
-Bill Cosby**

-Dedicated to my Father: Gregory Arzell Perry
6/29/16

## DEVIL'S ADVOCATE

Time creates distance, I invest years researching the
route

Please honor the family name, I will make my
father proud

Accept my position as a man, So I got shit to do

Princess Nyanna and Prince Zion I sacrifice it all
for you

Is it faith or temptation, what drive a man's will

Rejection is no accident, it only strengthens the deal

I inspire myself, But I acknowledge your belief

don't live for the opinions of others, So I refuse to
disappoint Me!

I doubted in the past, still haven't forgiven myself
for that

The structure of this family can no longer survive
on regret

Honor and obligation, my mission is much too important

I will not allow the values of my truth to be distorted

This poison has deeply penetrated our custom and culture

And shaken the very foundation of our family's infrastructure

I realized when my father passed that GOD had chosen me now

so, for the sake of this family, my mistakes cannot hold me down

**Confidence... thrives on honesty, on honor, on the sacredness of obligations, on faithful protection and on unselfish performance. Without them it cannot live.**
**-Franklin D. Roosevelt**

## RISE OF THE NEPHILLIM

I realized angels bring pleasure
Demons remind you of the pain
You don't know one without the other
This drives the weak insane
I learned to embrace the dark and the light
But it's an energy drain
Sometimes the pressure is hard to balance
I am Nephillim, so I maintain
My mission is to awaken my colleagues
We will defeat this distain

The future of humanity is at risk
And there have been too many lives slain.

*It is time to awaken, you have a mission*
*Time is growing short for you to accomplish what*
*you came to earth to do.*
*-Dolores Cannon*

## FEAR OF REJECTION (PART 1)

The strength of Acceptance
Replaces rejection,
Embracing the affection
a thought that's hesitation
feeling the gestation
giving birth to a relation,
Gotta learn to have patience
Is it worth all this waiting?
I'm just saying I've been praying
And I need to find a way in,
Tell her how I'm feeling
tell her what I'm seeing
I'm the thing that's missing
I'm the thing she's needing
but we're just being friendly

**A true friend is someone who lets you have total
freedom to be yourself - and specially to feel. Or, not
feel. Whatever you happen to be feeling now is fine
with them. That's what real love amounts to - letting
a person be what he really is.**
**-Jim Morrison**

## LOVES RULE, LIFE RULES (F.O.R #2)

In the lack of Affection, Love offers protection
Some peace comes at the price of rejection
But what about the question?
Was it true or obsession?
Why am I stressing over this confession?
I feel I have learned my lesson
But I am still
Trapped in rhythm and rhyme
Caught in this illusion of time
I convinced myself that I'd be fine
or maybe I'm just losing my mind
but if so, then why do I care
Why is the thought still there?
Why am I worried about my equal share?
Why does it seem that love/life can never play fair?

## NOT AGAIN!!!(F.O.R #3)

It's nice to see you my friend
I wondered how you had been
do you remember the times we spent?
when things were truly genuine
and not all about the dividends
Because I never had money to spend
to you that was a cardinal sin
Really, we never had time to begin
Without money, I knew it would end
So, my love I refused to send
I decided we should just stay friends
Because I cannot end up broken.... AGAIN!!

## MALNOURISHED (F.O.R. #4)

*Malnutrition or Malnourishment is a condition that results from eating a diet in which nutrients are either not enough or are too much such that the diet causes health problems.*

*-Wikipedia*

A ni\*\*a/ninja feels love deficient.
Shawty, what am I missing?
So full on promises that you are delivering
There is a diminishing return on my satisfaction
It's like you're associated with the wrong faction
This could be fixed but you lack action
Do you even know what I want?
because I hate asking,
If you're not ready for this, don't take the task then
My ego can't handle all this back tracking
Denial of self-pleasure is the ultimate sin
So, let's hold on baby, or we can start again
And if reset doesn't work, this will probably end
If you don't have enough love to give, don't pretend
I am malnourished and broken and I don't need
another friend.

## SECOND GUEST (MYSELF)

Are you sure you want to take on this role?

Or stand as a good example for those

Who you believe has a better chance for hope

But in the process, you sacrifice your ego

The very thing that always attracted the folk

That pointed you on the right path to go

This life has taught you many lessons before

You are who you are, and you can be no more

But your mind isn't clear,

undecided at the crossroad

Time doesn't exist until you make your vote

The universe doesn't care so just be bold

As this world change watch your life unfold

You chase your dreams because

you do what you are told

The things that you value in life are pointless

don't you know

Life will always be a process and not just a show

Many people have mistaken this wisdom for a joke

You were sent here to do a mission Not just chase

Goals.

But in the end, it's up to you the choice is yours I

suppose.

**The two major obstacles that stand in the way of achievement and success are fear and doubt**

**-Brian Tracy**

## I DOUBTED

I wanted to quit and let it all go
Take another path and choose another road
Give up on all of my dreams and all my hopes
And go on living life just like before
Nothing else to say nothing to show
Really, I don't want to perform anymore
My life has consequences too you know
So, my thoughts are not always exposed
There are things that I must keep down below
But for the sake of my family I choose to grow
I sometimes fear the transformation I must forgo
Because I have not yet reached my plateau
I still have not paid for all the sins I owe
And I have no more DOUBT in escrow
So Slowly through the troubles of life I float
I remember to live my life for ME also
Not for the fame, glory or Money, NO!
Either I love the things I do, or I Don't
Never again will I put my dreams on hold.

**Wise men, when in doubt whether to speak or to
keep quiet, give themselves the benefit of the
doubt, and remain silent
-Napoleon Hill**

## RAP VS POETRY

A disgrace of an art

I can't believe I gave birth to you

Once stood for something,

now you don't even have a clue

As I see what my child has become

I pray it's not true

But the time for your demise is long overdue

A virus to the minds of the youth,

you are becoming an issue

I brought you in to this world

and I'll use this pen to Undo

The mistakes cause by lack of intelligence from

fools

Art should be used to inspire not lower I.Q

Your place in this world will slowly become loose

There is no safety from my wrath I bid you ado

I thought I raised you right, but I guess I failed

The youth that practice your art

mostly end up jailed

Lives Corrupted, an entire race of people derailed

Whatever your purpose was I guess that shit bailed

I won't hold my tongue anymore this time I exhale

So, I'm taking shots prove yourself or be impaled

This pen is no joke and Poetry will prevail.

I remember rap music. We used to party and dance off of it. Today it's all about a whole different angle... Rappers are going against each other, and it's more of a bragging, boasting thing. What I'm trying to do is put back into rap music what's missing - which is the good part, the fun part, that party part.

*-Flavor Flav*

## HUMANITY'S LOVE LETTER

Are they not Human?
Do they no longer bleed?
Do they not love their families like me?
Are they not ambitious to chase their dreams?
 Do all they really seem to ask for is peace?
Are we not Human?
Is it not OK to disagree?
Is there a problem in what I choose to believe?
Can I not live the life I feel is for me?
Or Must I really compete with loved ones
economically?
We Are Human
No one should go hungry we all should eat
Love me no matter what religion I preach
We all have pride in our Nation At least
Overcome our childish ways for the sake of
Humanity!

**Love and compassion are necessities, not
Luxuries. Without them Humanity cannot
survive.
-Dalai Lama**

**Birth of a Nephilim (Miscellaneous notes)**

- Don't Let your Learning lead to knowledge you'll become a fool, Let your learning lead to action
- You can waste time learning become very smart and broke
- Find out how things work and work it don't try to beat it.
- The ways I don't try to be is me and those that know and understand will respect it.
- We are still learning this dimension, the 3$^{rd}$ dimension, learning duality in the second dimension the good vs bad. As we learn the dimensional rules of this spectrum of the universe, we see we become more unified. We've always only looked at two perspectives of any issue which is funny because in a 3d realm we need to learn depth or to be deeper.
- Life is full of permutations and combinations. Sometimes the order you do things matter sometimes it doesn't, but in order to find the solution in life you must

work through each possibility presented to find your opportunity.

- When you hear GOD's voice it's fast almost instant knowledge, but you don't understand it.
- Leaders don't think like followers, we think a lot more!
- Pay attention to the body, it's alive and it notices you and your choices. It notices and has an individual personality as a mass whole and an individual. All the choices you make benefit you in the same way. Learn to focus the mind on hearing the pleas of the entire body not just the selfish ones.


- I'd rather do different things the same way than the same thing different ways.
- Jail isn't to punish the bad because there is no such thing. It's population control to keep genes out of the gene pool or kill traditions and rewrite history
- `The pineal Gland or the 3rd eye leads to spiritual Guidance and Ideas. It produces

melatonin when it's awakened. There is a slight pressure at the back of the neck, and you can feel sleepy or dazed like you are fading from reality it could also lead to sleep. You see inside of your head, not out of it.

- Most ideas, thoughts are not your own, determine who you are first before you determine who you want to be.

- The weaker your mind the more life gets to you. Your mental strength is your peace of mind, beyond believing in faith, KNOWING the truth. You cause yourself to experience what you need to do in order to get what you want. The more you keep changing your mind the more your life will keep changing. Keep focused on what you want. Act upon it when it's urged by the deep inner you.

- The Sabbath isn't a day for GOD but a day for you, to break the illusion and the reality that is what you are creating. The Sabbath is a holy day because it's a day taken to rest from your creative energy and your world to remember who you are. Rest your mind, rest your soul, and rest your body Heaven is when every day is the Sabbath.

- Life isn't a trial but more of a show or performance. In the end you will see how spectacular you were, you will be your own judge in life, will you be impressed.

- They are not commandments but Commitments, the commandments are not laws you must follow to get to heaven but when you realize that you are already following them they are signs that you are already in heaven.

- The idea that GOD is only one individual being is Impossible to me. One being alone can never maintain the intricate process that collectively we all refer to as GOD, or the Life process. GOD isn't a BEING we speak with but a PROCESS that all beings obey. How do you define your own choices? Ultimately GOD is simply our Operating system!!

- A program or Being that doesn't obey its natural operating process is in given many names, virus, cancers, alien, foreign, demon, devil, Bad, Dark, etc... GOD is a behavior. Every behavior is important to the entire function of GOD; therefore, every behavior is necessary. Every process needs a balance to work properly.

- Anyone can dream... That's easy. I know anything is possible, do not make plans based on what's possible. You get lost in dreams that way. Make plans based on what is PROBABLE!

- "GOD" cannot be aware of itself, based on universal law. It's the same restriction we all have. In order to achieve self-awareness "GOD" must be experienced. In order to experience everything "GOD" divided into Infinity. Every individual part of infinity is an experience of "GOD" we also are branches of that "Divinity" or "Divided Infinity" as I like to call it.

- I am aware that everyone that exists has a story, and we all exist because that story is important for us to tell. We should choose to live our lives nobly with understanding that if you exist your story is just as important to this world as mine and we all have the rights to live and tell the most important story we have ever known the story of our existence.

- To be honest I feel that GOD is only one of MANY discoveries of experience we will have. Once GOD is figured out it won't be a big deal anymore and we will need another puzzle to solve in experience.

- Life is a pattern, at one level of magnification we can see individuals experiencing Good and Bad Possibilities, but on a different level of looking at it this can be seen as Balance, or Homeostasis. Without this equilibrium of good and bad experiences the entire system of life cannot stay balanced.

- I believe the war against the police and the war against black men is being propagated and is a controlled conflict of the illuminati or whoever the real ruling class is. It is still population control, history being written on purpose, the easiest way to mark the targets. Police officers regardless of race are expendable, cheap soldiers paid less than the military to start local controlled conflicts. This helps with distraction and diversion tactics and placing the police force in the public eye as the new scape goats to blame. They are just as much pawns in the overall game as we all are.

## MY FIGHTING SPIRIT

*Do not place hope in finding a secret technique. Polish the mind through ceaseless training that is the key to effective techniques.*

    *-Kyuzo Mifune*

1. Work On developing new Close quarter trapping style: Including Judo Throws, Tai-Chi Chin-na, Army MMA, Eagle Claw, Wing Chun, Baji-Quan,
2. Hammer blows to body and limbs pressure points instead of punching using less energy
3. Restrain one's self and yield to others not because one is weak, but to uphold the ethical Tao and let the others have their claim.
4. "Control yourself; let others do what they will. This does not mean you are weak. Control your heart, obey the principles of life. This does not mean others are stronger."

*On the highest level, an opponent is allowed to tire himself out, evasion becoming the key defense. Energy control is highly developed,*

*and the degree to which the body must be*
*moved to redirect or avoid impact is under*
*greater control.*

1. Focus to train and condition the body.
2. Be righteous and uphold your honor.
3. Respect parents, honor teachers.
4. Treat others with honesty; treat your friends with loyalty.
5. Rely on a variety of fighting techniques that can be employed for a wide range of needs.

## TOUGH VS TRAINED A MILITARY MIND

The art of fighting to me is a very powerful and spiritual experience, when fully understood fighting can be a very good stress reliever and sometimes it can help a person develop a better understanding of one's mind and body a respect for natural and universal laws and even a very good bonding experience depending on the situations involved within each fighter. In order to be considered a fighter a person simply chooses to be one and in return focuses some of their time to develop their own understanding of what the human body can really do. My understanding and respect for fighting came at an early age as I have been in physical combat with other people since the age of 7 years old. Early on in those days my experience with combat and fighting was a fearful event, it was forced upon me to defend myself and it is also where I noticed my power and the energies involved when in fight mode. Being born in poverty creates situations where only the strongest will survive and eat. I was naïve at this time because I was born with a loving and noble spirit, fighting was against my natural feelings and I had not learned the energy control needed for self-combat and defense. In my first few attempts at combat I had no idea what I was supposed to be feeling or thinking, I had no clue about the dangers of a fight or being in a hostile situation. One of the things I want to point out is that lack of fighting experience can really hinder a fighter from reaching his true potential as a matter of fact my belief is that it's the fighting experience itself that earns you the ranks of improvement. No amount of studying, reading or watching combat can give you the experience that one single fight, (win or lose) can teach any fighter and that experience is necessary for development. As a child, I learned these lessons early as my combat record has twice as many losses as wins. Regardless of age if a person could kick your ass you respected and obeyed them unless you were willing to challenge them.

Once I joined the military and started basic training I was once again in a situation where fighting was how you earned respect in the barracks. The base in South Carolina is considered EASY by some veterans compared to many other bases and I'm sure they are but you must still realize it is a military base and the interactions are nothing short of the shenanigans many people have described before. My story is not the hardest of military fight stories, but it is one none the less. I figured the first job of the military was to scare and break you down mentally and going into the situation fully aware to what they were going to do I did enjoy myself. I had already been through a very tough childhood in poverty and had survived a lot of crazy situations, so I wasn't really affected by the military like most people. They truly couldn't handle it and even in a light base like ours people washed out and had to go home to their loving parents. I never had parents, so I was in no hurry to go back home the military was an enjoyable time for me. At night is when most of the action happened. The drill Sargent would go home and Lock us up in the bay, it was about 60 of us in there we were directly across from the girls which is another story entirely. There was an alarm on the door, so we could not leave, and no one could enter until morning. Many nights we would have moonlight fights in the middle of the bay but mostly it was all in good fun. We were raging with testosterone and no one could really sleep until we burned off all of that energy. Like I said Most of the fights were harmless displays of toughness from each represented neighborhood in each respectable state and city. From California to New York I was the only one from Atlanta GA go figure we all had a certain level of respect we had to gain, and we did not want to dishonor where we were from. In these fights, I held my respectable own with my grapple style Hybrid Judo Wrestling. I never threw a punch though. I witness locking styles, striking styles and other forms of street fighting. But none of us were ready for what the drill sergeant introduced us to. A recruit, a military brat who was forced into service from his Sargent Major father and he had been a trained militant since birth. His approach to the group was very hostile and he was there to play no games. He wanted out and he was willing to break rules because he knew the system and he didn't fear it. He wasn't afraid of the toughest person we had in our ranks. He was TRAINED as he would state it and he intended to prove that on us. We would be the focus of his pent-up aggression and it took an entire platoon full of military recruits to take out one guy, He would become my first nemesis

One night as we all gathered the pillows on the middle of the ground for cushion and then use our Flashlights for illumination because turning on the lights would alert CQ and therefore alarm the drill sergeant. We would all lie in our bunks facing the center floor and two willing fighters would hop off the beds and prepared to bout. After watching like two fights one of my closest friends at the time let's call him Tyrel wanted to go out for some fun. Tyrel wasn't really from anywhere particular, no family moved state to state he joined to find structure and get off the streets. He was skinny but very chill guy, funny even at times he boxed mostly from a gym he trained at while he was in New York somewhere. Unknowingly to any of us of his abilities the new recruit jumps off the bed with a sinister grin and states he wants to play too. Let's call this Guy Mike, he was very dark skinned but American no doubt he never discloses anything about his back ground or where he's from he's about 6 feet maybe even 5'10 to 5 '11 but not very tall. He had an athletic physic and he seemed to be angry most of the time. I felt un easy about the fight, but My friend was too much a laid-back guy to pay attention. You can tell he wasn't joking around like the rest of us. As the sparring started, they both took boxing stances with fist out front, they circled each other and traded a few body blows and block jabs nothing too serious. The guys who were holding the lights started horse playing and there were periods of sheer blackness followed by glimpses of the two recruits. We taunted for them to cut it out or we were going to call it a night and all go to bed. In a very moment that the lights had flickered off my friend Tyrel and Mike we all heard a loud Crack sound and everyone panicked and said shine the lights on the floor bro Shine the damn lights!!, My friend Tyrel Lay on the ground with a bloody mouth and Mike standing over him We all rushed in and me and a few boys grabbed Tyrel and went into the Bay restroom at the back. Others grabbed Mike as if to hold him back, but he wasn't struggling or even resisting just smiling. We dragged Tyrel in the showers and begin rinsing the blood away and waking him up. We were very scared of getting into trouble, I could hear the others questioning MIKE back in the bay, but my focus was making sure Tyrel was ok. As he woke up, I asked Very Angrily Bro what the hell did he hit you with, did he have something in his hand. Tyrel had a split eye and lip he was hit TWICE. Tyrel responded he hit me with his Fist man. Bullshit!! I didn't believe it, I stormed out of the bathroom and headed straight for Mike, but a group of recruits grabbed me and when Mike saw me coming, he came towards me taunting me as he really didn't care what he had done. The soldiers in the bay held us back from each other and then Tyrel came out of the bathroom and said Willis don't man, this dude is crazy or something. Mike smirked and said listen to your boy, then he went on to rave again about his military troubles and how he has been trained by his father since he was a boy and he would knock anyone of us out if he had to he didn't believe he could get into trouble because of his father. Another recruit who had been watching the entire thing was getting impatient with Mike's talking we called this guy Lurch he was very tall and slim he had never gotten into an incident with anyone, but he spoke up now. Lurch said he was tired of listening to Mike talk shit and he needed to shut his mouth. Mike walked over to lurch as he was lying on the side of the top bunk and said who's going to make me shut up and then out of nowhere, he proceeded to Punch Lurch extremely hard and we all heard this one too. Lurch's body had gone relaxed his hand and head dropped and hang off the bed and blood dripped from his top lip, he was out cold. This was too much for one recruit who immediately ran towards the door to get help from CQ about 8 soldiers rushed towards Mike to take him down, the door had been opened now the alarm was ringing the sergeants are on their way but we all wanted payback first. Mike held his own before we could take him down even as I rush him to grab him his punch connected perfectly on my jaw and I was stunned. I never got a chance to get at him again by the time I got back to my feet at least 3 of us were getting up the rest were holding him down and the sergeants were finally coming to take care of our little problem. They walked him away as he continued running his mouth, we all went to clean up before heading back to bed. We never seen Mike again but soon after that we started Close combat training and because of my incident I have focused on defending myself since then, I was tough, but Mike was clearly trained.

## SCORPION KUNG FU:
## ONE OF THE 5 DEADLY VENOMS OF
## MARTIAL ARTS

**Scorpion kung Fu-** The scorpion represents a double threat. Kicks from the Scorpion style are just like the stinging tail of the namesake. When delivered by a master, a single kick can paralyze or even kill, let alone the strong pincer-style attack of the arms to contend with. The weakness in this style is not clearly revealed it would be to stay out of reach of The Scorpion's damaging kicks and make him come to you.

There are various hand trapping and immobilizing techniques that can be utilized in the trapping range. An opponent's attempt at blocking a strike can be turned into a devastating trap. Traps can cross an opponent's hands, in a manner where they cannot continue to block. These types of traps can be seen especially in Wing Chun and Jeet Kune Do Hand trapping can be followed by some type of muscle or nerve destruction. This can be done by attacking inherent vulnerabilities in the construction of human hands and arms. Hand trapping skills can be important to offset an opponent's blocks. An opponent's block is sometimes referred to as an obstruction. Fighters well versed in the trapping range learn techniques that will remove these obstructions or go around them. This training enables a fighter to strike their opponent while immobilizing their arms. Effective traps are ones that tie up an opponent's two arms while utilizing just one of your own

My scorpion style fighting starts with its ROOTS as a grappling style more than striking, since that is where my roots started, and my instinct is to get close and get my hands on the opponent. I have seen other "scorpion styles but they are mainly focused on striking and seem to have very complex body positioning and very dynamic move sets. My style is based on the combination of the basics of a few styles and tries not to be as complex as the other scorpion styles. I tried to integrate wrestling as the basic grappling style, but this did not flow very well with my body size, wrestling is based on strength and power something I was not born with a lot of. Even through the years of resistance training

I could never gain the muscles or the body of a heavy weight wrestler, so I looked for other styles of grappling until I discovered JUDO. My first love, with its basis in balance, weigh control, leverage and positioning many JUDO throws can be executed with little Strength and if the technique is mastered the opponent literally throws themselves this replaced my wrestling. Once the opponent is in the RED ZONE, close ranged or grapple zone for the sake of positioning. The standard Judo throws apply, the lock you are looking for is the left-hand locks right wrist and right-hand lock back of the head putting Pressure on the neck points on each side, or if the opponent is larger and has on a shirt go for standard Judo Grapple of the collar. If opponent is very larger and unable to gain grapple advantage of then you need to chisel him down with Medium to heavy strikes to the body and legs before going for a high-risk grapple opportunity. This is where Pressure points and strike attacks became a necessity of the style and it could not stay a Grapple only style, I'm not always able to gain a knockout blow but I need each blow to count somehow or I'll waste energy. I started studying the

Body and its weakness. There is No technique that is perfect for all situations, what you do depends on what your opponent does, you must adapt to fit the circumstances. I have learned that attacking some pressure points are more affective if you take your opponent by surprise. Once the opponent becomes aware of your intent, if they are strong, they can mentally block or reduce the effect of the pressure point strike. This does not mean that the strike will not cause them damage, but you could lose the advantage or be forced to go on defense if you are in an improper position or have left yourself vulnerable because you anticipated a follow-up or finishing strike. If this happens and you can continue the fight you may be forced to use a more effective pressure point strike or limb twist or breaking attack to disable the opponent. For me, the opponents LIMBS are my first opponent. I like to disable the ability to strike effectively before I attempt a high-risk finisher technique. Fights are fast, and most opponents take a considerable amount of damage to slow or stop them. I have seen fights where a person only attacked once, and when it did not work, they were completely out of ideas.

Even If you study the arts or prefer instinctual street fighting, the first thing I have learned is to never UNDERESTIMATE your opponent or their abilities. It is the first and only mistake you may be allowed to make. A lot of fights end quickly, but if your opponent is ready for combat, the fight could physically last for quite some time if uninterrupted. If there is a second lesson, I have learned it would be ACCEPT YOUR SITUATION. Many fights will catch you off guard, a lot of people may sucker punch or attempt a cheap shot before you are even aware you are in a fight. If you even FEEL as if you are in a hostile situation, BE ON GUARD. Accept the situation and become very serious, you could be in danger and this is not the time to doubt yourself regardless of your skill level or mastery. You cannot simply choose a technique to use in a fight because a fight is dynamic, and its flow is usually always unpredictable. But if you are aware of a select number of techniques for various situations, also aware of when to execute those techniques and how to apply them you will be a much more effective fighter. I think this was BRUCE LEE meaning of "Be Like Water". Many people fight and have a static set of techniques they will attempt to gain glory by trying to perform. By not trying to INTENTIONALLY fight and harm another person you should seek no glory. In my opinion, a fight is justified in defense of yourself or the greater good of the situation at hand. Judgements must always be made and we each can only hope that we made correct ones when it was needed. Ultimately, we only have our principles and what we stand for to judge any decision by. Try not to advertise your techniques too much by being flashy, remember the theory is to try to surprise your opponent with each technique you perform, hide them in normal movements. Don't always aim for PERFECTION in your performance of a technique, as stated before a fight is fast and positions change quickly, once you decide on a technique and it becomes LOADED. Execute it the best way you can, even a POORLY executed technique can have more of an effect than you may believe, also it helps you to understand how to perform that technique in real time and your confidence to perform and remember it during future fights with expand. I believe a fighter needs to understand the art of controlling the situation and the MIND and ATTENTION of his opponent. I believe this helps to control position and the tempo giving you the advantage and forcing your opponent to play CATCH-UP. The battle for position and location in a fight is just as important as each technique attempted. The way I see it the person that controls the location and position of the fight also controls and limits the type of techniques their opponent can perform from that position. You can give yourself an advantage while at the same time putting them at a big disadvantage simply because of where you are standing in relation to them. Simple techniques are usually faster and easier to apply, as we get older, we can lose speed and mobility but we gain wisdom, so I learned to fight Smarter not harder than the opponent. The human body has its limits and rules that no one can change, each joint and limb only need a certain amount of pressure at a certain angle to become disabled. There are certain POINTS on the body that cannot be trained. They are vital they are deadly, and they do not need a lot of energy to strike and be effective. Pain controls a person more than they may know people want to hurt you in a fight, but never anticipate being hurt. Many attackers only have an intent to do harm. They seek pleasure more than avoiding pain. In a defensive style, I would rather avoid pain than seek pleasure. So, most of the attacks are counter attacks and capture grabs. I consider different things when I try to describe my style. I often enjoyed the Asian arts and I understand how the arts have been derived from African culture in one way or another. Not to disrespect any master of any culture I also considered African fighting historically and many African masters explained fighting arts dating back to the spear and Shield days.

## Pressure Point Locations

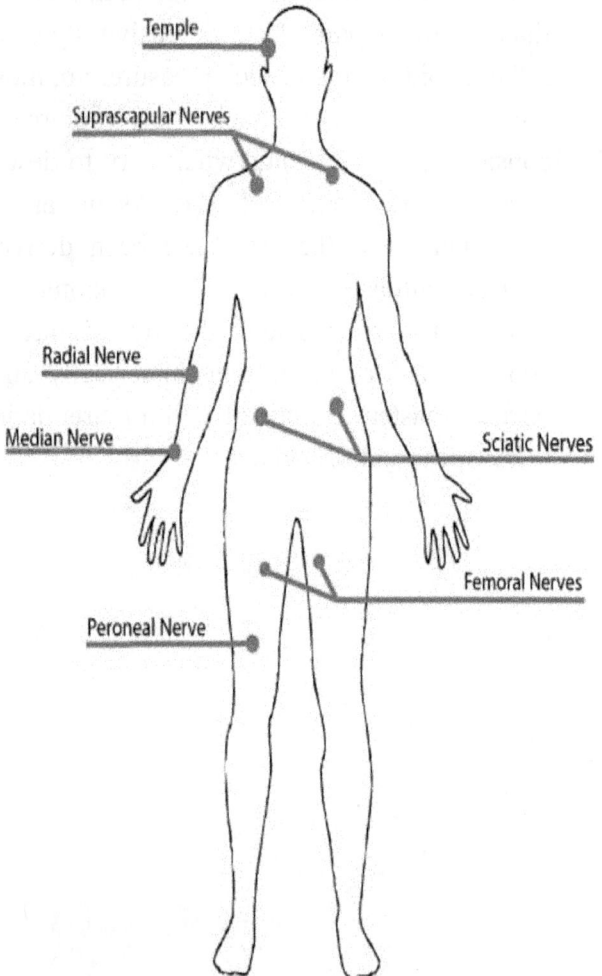

Temple
Suprascapular Nerves
Radial Nerve
Median Nerve
Sciatic Nerves
Femoral Nerves
Peroneal Nerve

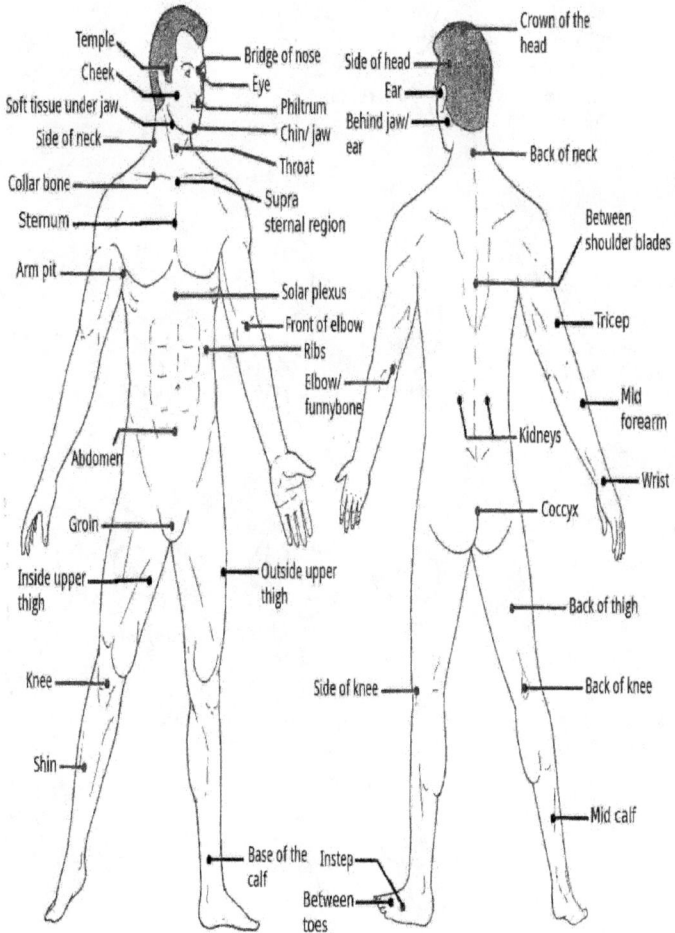

Temple

Cheek

Soft tissue under jaw

Side of neck

Collar bone

Sternum

Arm pit

Abdomen

Groin

Inside upper thigh

Knee

Shin

Base of the calf

Bridge of nose

Eye

Philtrum

Chin/ jaw

Throat

Supra sternal region

Solar plexus

Front of elbow

Ribs

Elbow/ funnybone

Outside upper thigh

Instep

Between toes

Crown of the head

Side of head

Ear

Behind jaw/ ear

Back of neck

Between shoulder blades

Tricep

Mid forearm

Kidneys

Wrist

Coccyx

Back of thigh

Back of knee

Side of knee

Mid calf

ippon nukite    empi    uraken seiken ude tetsui    keito    washide

nihon nukite    teisho    seryuto    kumade    kakuto

haito shuto haishu    ippon ken    nakadaka ken    hiraken    yonhon nukite

hiza    haisoku    koshi kakato    sokuto    teisoku

## SENPAI AND SENSEI

***Scott Rogers (Pressure Points) - Taught*** from hands-on experience, not theory. Rogers is a 4th Dan Black Belt Master Rank in Okinawan Kempo and an expert in Kyushojutsu. He has also attained a 3rd Dan Black Belt in Korean Taekwondo, 1st Dan Black Belt in Japanese Taijutsu. Rogers has also cross trained in several other arts, most notably western boxing and Wing Chun Kung Fu.

***Master Wong (Wing Chun) -*** With a mixed heritage of Chinese and Vietnamese and living in North Vietnam he was forced to fight for food at a young age. Also, being a mixed race, this was frowned upon and with heavy racism you could easily be killed for just being born. A mysterious old man who lived next to him taught him a little martial art but after being forced out of Vietnam and moving to the UK he was kicked out of school for fighting and finally at the age of 15 found his master who remains unnamed and started his official Martial arts training.

***Karo Parisian (No GI Judo)*** - Parisyan was born in Yerevan, Armenia. His family migrated to America when he was six years old. Parisyan started training in judo when he was nine years old, Parisyan stated that his father began taking him to judo lessons because he beat up on his sisters and judo would be an effective outlet for Parisyan to take out his anger. For more than thirteen years, Parisyan developed under the Hayastan Grappling System, which blends elements of Judo, Sambo, Catch Wrestling, Greco-Roman and Freestyle wrestling. Parisyan has six Junior National belts to his credit and competed in the Olympic Judo trials ahead of the 2004 games in Athens. He wrote that going to the Olympics was his dream and that mixed martial arts was only an outlet for his boredom.

***Rhadi Ferguson (Judo2004)*** - Ferguson grew up in Miami, Florida in the United States where he began training in judo at the age of 7 Ferguson is a four-time national champion in judo. At the age of 29, Ferguson competed in judo at the 2004 Summer Olympics in Athens, Greece in the men's heavyweight division In addition to judo, Ferguson also holds a black belt in Brazilian jiu-jitsu, and has competed in numerous jiu-jitsu and submission grappling tournaments.

***Bruce Lee-(Philosophy)*** - Bruce Lee's martial art could not have been as successful and complete without the deep philosophical base he gave it. Taoist philosophy is the development of the Chinese sage Lao Tzu, who in the sixth century BC wrote the definitive work on the subject, the Tao Te Ching. Bruce would have a great epiphany. "On the sea, I thought of all my past training and got mad at myself and punched the water. Right then at that moment, a thought suddenly struck me. Wasn't this water the essence of gung fu? I struck it, but it did not suffer hurt. I then tried to grasp a handful of it but it was impossible. This water, the softest substance, could fit into any container. Although it seemed weak, it could penetrate the hardest substance. That was it! I wanted to be like the nature of water. "Therefore, in order to control myself I must accept myself by going with, and not against, my nature.

*__Yang Jwing-Ming-(Taiji Chi-Na)__ -* Born in 1946 in the republic of China he started training at age 15 in Shaolin White Crane and White Crane Chin-Na through massage and herbal treatment. Eventually Dr. Yang taught college level Martial arts in the united stated while studying Physics and engineering but eventually gave up his career to focus on teaching and studying the arts.

*__Troy J Price- (Fight flow)-__* Troy J. Price began his Karatedo and Kobudo training in 1982 at the Columbia School of Karatedo West Columbia, SC, under the direction of **Hanshi Ridgely Abele**. In 1985 he began studying Ju-Jutsu along with his Karatedo training. In 1997 he also began studying Baguazhang and Qigong and in 1999 began studying Taijiquan and Xingyiquan. Mr. Price trains with several nationally and internationally known instructors in the traditional Martial Arts of Karatedo, Ju-Jutsu, Kobudo, Aikido, Kyusho-Jutsu, Judo, Chin-Na, Wing Chun, Baguazhang, Xingyiquan, Taijiquan and Qigong.

***Kyuzo Mifune- (Airplane throw) (Philosophy)*** -
has been categorized as one of the greatest
exponents of the art of judo after the founder, Kanō
Jigorō. He is considered by many to be the greatest
judo technician ever, after Kanō.

holding

naked strangle

major outer reaping throw

sweeping hip throw

major inner reaping throw

stomach throw

arm lock

one-arm shoulder throw

## THOUGHTS TO MYSELF

Ok I decided to keep I guess a journal or should I say diary of some of the zany things me and myself and sometimes I would talk about, of course ME being the outer me, MYSELF being my spirit or middle me and I or some call him I AM or my soul or subconscious even some call it GOD, but I just call him I. Um, I feel in the even this is used as evidence for my conviction into the Looney bin or crazy house I guess my final words to society would be... HI MOM!! Look I made it on TV. Ok let's be serious.

I think I had my first comprehensible conversation with I and here is what I had a chance to write down. I bought this journal for that reason. I really hope it turns out to be a best seller. I will be recording all my conversations and thoughts with all 3 of my inner selves for a month... Here is Number 1

When challenged with a decision to lie to a friend about a certain situation I turned to myself to give me advice. Now first I should explain the connection between the 3. Me- is the outer self the physical. Myself- is the middle or the bridge between the deep inner and the most outer Me. Because myself is the medium it becomes my Medium or channel or energy used to communicate to higher knowledge. Myself is always subject to suggestion and opinions but all major decision should be made by I. So, most of the time it's me and myself making most decisions and moving about everyday life, but sometimes I speak, and it comes through myself directly to me. You see it's up to Me to carry out the actions that I want. Ok so Again here is the conversation about lying, lies and a lie.

+ Me- What is a lie?

+ I- A false image in the brain, deception in guidance towards a goal, you lie first on the inside. You create that possibility and when you accept it, it lives and becomes reality.

+ Me- Is Lying Bad?

+ I- No, lying is neither good or bad it just is your intentions behind how you use it is the only thing that matters

+ Me—why do we hate lying so much?

+ I- People are lost and need direction. Be it a big deal or not it's promotes distrust when you throw yourself or someone else off their spiritual and physical path. But the main person hurt by lies is the teller.

+ Me- Is Lying Good?

+ I- it can be, sometimes people can't see past their reality. So, you can create one for them with a lie. Force them to see what they can't,

they will think you're a nice but you're just
a good liar.

+ Me- So is this how fortune teller tells your
future and past?

+ I- those people probably use a combination
of both brain functions. Logic to see past
and present and insight and spirit to read
possible futures they are never wrong
because all is possible, everyone can do this.

+ Me- So Wait, I can do that but wouldn't that
be wrong?

+ I- depending on your intentions and
competencies
Intention is spirit, competency is logic,
Intentions go off a feeling, and no one can
give them to you. It's your true power to
intend your true freedom to intend. How
competent you are will help you judge
physical patterns. Talking and listening to

people when your logical and competency skills are high will result in possible past and present visions in the mind.

+ Me- So when should I use lies Vs. Truth?

+ I- You already know when, you should lie to the homeless man on the street and tell him you just had a vision that they will get better. Tell the truth when true guidance is needed or desired. Tell the truth as much as possible to stay true to "MYSELF" or yourself I should say. Whatever you send through myself the medium to I the inner, I will accept as a request and give myself Ideas to pass to make it real. Lies should be used with caution because I will begin to make them real for ME.

+ Me- How do I know you are real?

- I- I am not and never will be. I am you and everyone else. I am real every day but not in the way you understand yet.
- Me- why don't you listen?
- I- I should ask you the same. I am always talking but I stopped when my opinions were no longer needed, same as you would. I cannot control free will, so I shut up. Do as you will I could care less.
- Me- Really? Careless, what about this love stuff?
- I- I do love you because you are me, I must I am love but it's not my life it's yours I already gave it to you. I don't take back my gifts. Lol
- Me- Are you the devil?
- I- what is the devil? A humanoid creature that's ugly… well to some and he lies which we already talked about. I am who you want

me to be if evil is what you want, I'll flood you with bad Ideas.

Me- OK since you are clearly not ME can you answer something I don't know?

I- No, but I can help you answer it yourself

Me- But I thought you were all knowing?

I- Not through you alone but the collection of experiences from everything I AM.

Me- Ok so why do we sleep, dream and why can't I remember?

I- that's easy and you have already been given the answer before you asked, right?

Me- yes, it's weird

I- so write it down

Me- "Ok, no one can explain sleep or dreams because its intent wasn't a physical thing. Physically it converts experiences and knowledge to memory but what does that mean. It means direct communication with source or

Me or you or however you put it. It's inner
reflection and in the morning every morning
there should be direction in either way good or
bad depending on Perspective of life."
It was clear that I Assumed I was talking to
GOD I mean the GOD from back in the church
days GOD but being skeptic, I started to worry
if I was losing it or was, I ok. I once again
reflected inside for the answer.

In my Journey's through myself and in my head, I have discovered so many wonderful Ideas and throughout the years I have been given so many thoughts that still haven't even been accepted by other people. All of them original in nature to some extent and I have written them all down. No, I have never attempted to do any of these things yet but this book along with so many other Ideas I will be trying out in years to come. I have been given a glimpse of a possible future and been told all I must do is listening and follow. The crazy thing is I have no idea how it will all come to past if any of it ever happen, but my life will be the experiment. Maybe I'm getting ahead of myself in telling you what I want you to know. So, as we get into the lessons, I will give you the thoughts from me the outer and deeper thoughts from I come through myself. Ok one of the first lessons I taught myself is how do I get motivated. How do I get started? I wanted to explain this to myself in a very simple and logical way as I am still learning spiritual awakening. As I thought to myself or talked to myself a few simple words came to me. They are Sleep, Fun, and Inspiration, creation, living and changing. Now at first me and myself did not fully understand what I was trying to tell me. So, I meditated, now some of the techniques that I use or the journey I went through to discover how to hear and recognize your inner voice I will not disclose. Not because I cannot but because it's not important at least not to me. There are plenty of books and people and even websites and movies that can all give you guidance on how to reach your higher self. This is simply a journal on our conversations. Ok so like I said I meditated, now as I got deeper into my subconscious, I found myself and asked for clearer guidance to words. The true meaning of what I wanted, why did I give myself these words to pass to me? Slowly as I held the question, thoughts, Ideas, and a voice answered. It was I talking to me. Now remember I was asked by me a question of how I start creating the simple logical way. Now let's break down each word and sum up the lesson I wanted to teach me. Sleep- or Meditate- Sleep itself is direct communication with self. It is inner reflection, when you have absolutely no idea how to make a move in your life I recommend going to sleep and meditate or think. The body and mind are already at rest and if you focus at the major times of the day when you already sleepy it is easy for you to see clearly what you want but that's just the beginning of creation, we still have a few more words in the cycle that need clarity.

Next on the list is FUN, now this came as a surprise as fun was never a word that traditional churches or religions preached when it came to know yourself or GOD. GOD seemed boring and lame and if he was a human, I probably wouldn't be his friend. I felt that I only liked him because I had no other choice, or he'd turn me into salt or burn me in fire. I didn't want that, so I obeyed with boring accuracy. But fun, it was different almost everything I knew that was fun was bad for you in some way or the other. But I was reminded that bad is a perspective and then I was given the deepness of fun.

After SLEEP has brought you a vision or dream or idea or possibility you need to find the fun in it. If you can't, make it up and put fun in it, I loves fun and I will increase my Ideas 10x's over if I can have fun in what I do. You see me and myself realized the people having the fun are happy and healthy because I want to maintain that fun, even sick people get better when you inject fun. It's candy for the soul and I love it. Too much can cause cavities but managed well fun is exactly what everyone needs. So, put fun in your vision after sleep.

Now as weird as it sounds all this information hit
me instantly and I had never written it down until
now. I completely understand all the concepts as
soon as I gave them to myself. I am hoping they
also work for whoever reads this.

Now next in the creation process that came to me
was inspiration, now this one was hard because I am
not easily inspired by many things, my arrogance
makes me hard to please. To be inspired by
something it should touch my spirit at least. If you
have an Idea and see the fun in it being inspired by
it should be the easiest part. But When I turned to
myself for inspiration I was bombarded with the
complete opposite. I was given doubt, worry, fear,
impatience and frustration, I was afraid that myself
wouldn't like the idea. But to be inspired you must
place the idea in yourself for others. Really, I didn't
care much of how others felt so I turned to myself
now since myself is the medium between I and me

and a bridge for all spiritual suggestion. It is very compassionate. I realized all the emotions that were bombarding me were not from me but others. The fact that I had accepted the idea it became a future, possible reality and these were feelings from other people who were willing to try my idea but if I never added inspiration in the mix the feedback was coming in negative. Myself didn't like it and soon as I realized it I knew that success in any Idea comes from inspiring others. So, I had to find a way to make sure what I was going to create was fun and it inspired people to create their own either versions of my idea or something original.

Now creation is the part I am at now and hopefully by the time anyone is reading this I'll be at the next level. Creation is really the hard part for most of us because it involves doing and it seems like everything, I have a great Idea It's me who does all the work creating it. Creation is the physical energy needed to bring or manifest your creation in your experience or life. It's the meat and potatoes of creation. It can be done through hard work or paid labor or several literally hundreds of humanly known actions either good or bad depending on idea and execution. Simply put it must be done. Like writing this journal when I'd much rather be drinking, hanging with girls, and eating or something else. Now I realize that this part can be discouraging because truthfully, we as people want our fun and inspiration and ideas to be here now. I want to enjoy it now, not spend years creating just to fail. But I reassured myself that this is just the way it is. I cannot control the laws governing our universe and one of them is time. I realized every word I write everything is creation, like cells in the body it takes trillions of individual cells to come together as a whole to make me. A book takes hundred and thousands of individual spots of ink on a page in the form of letters to form words and words form books. Everything has its process in this world, even as powerful as I am, I still take 9 months of your time with your rules to even make you. In my mind, I was created as soon as I became a possibility, I became a reality so here I am stuck in the creative process. It's not fun now I tell you but I have faith everything starts at the simplest point the most basic and grows into something more complicated over time if continued to be worked on and the more time invested in an idea it becomes more and more perfect until it reaches its max potential before it changes into something different maintaining all the greatest qualities it had before and only adding greatness to it. Example, this book as I said starts from sentences; they form paragraphs which form pages. The sum of the pages makes a book and the collection of the same or similar information in a collection of books is a volume and a city where different and diverse books live and maintain their daily everyday job and life is a library. But all of them started as a single thought including this one.

After creation comes the best part. Living, once your creation is in your reality what good is it if you don't give it the breath of life and live it. All things desire to be used otherwise they are useless. This seems simple, right? Wrong, people don't get it and it's the best part. Live your creation, be it good or bad you are impacting something deeper. Living your creation attracts the rewards that you deserve and should be blessed with because you devoted your un-returnable time. A Lot of the blessings these days come in the form of money or material things. I will talk about these later but for now know that earning a reward and not accepting it makes ME mad. With all the work me, myself and I put into creating it at least let me enjoy it. You

should live it also because your living it attracts
people who are seeking inspiration like you once
were and on the cycle of creation, living your life
through your creation gives the original inspiration
you added to your creation to be absorbed into the
spirit and sometimes the soul of the audience your
creation was made for. Now many people make it to
this point although I'm not there yet but there is one
more crucial step that I wanted me to know and it's
changing or continued growth. That part is
important.

Changing, now like the butterfly and probably
hundreds of other things in nature, we must change.
For those of you with a higher conscience you
probably already know why, growth. As beautiful
as something is, it is never better than what it is
becoming. To think about it, nothing that evolved
was for the worse and always got better for
whatever it was that changed, Cars, computers,

food, animals, people, kids, whatever everything gets better so growth is needed. Think movement more than growth if you like. Does that mean stick with an idea until its perfect? NO WAY! If you're done with a creation give it back to nature, its natural course in its life will take over and it will continue to grow if necessary, through the ideas and input of others. It may evolve into something else or it may die if not needed anymore once you give an idea back to nature, move on and don't dwell. If you raised, you baby well enough it will live on for as long as it possibly can. If your idea dies you can resurrect it, but the key point is change. Do not get comfortable in success if it leads to that. Keep growing with new ideas; you must keep growing and moving. What happens to anything that doesn't grow and change with the masses? Matter is constantly changing without change or growth the negative energy catches up to your ideas and you.

Negative energy has been attributed to misunderstandings, deformities, failure, and death of a creation. We are all running from this energy until we have enough light or great ideas to beat this energy so in the meantime change and movement will keep you from being swallowed by negative energy. Simply out, stay busy. Now these five or should I say six virtues I guess would be their title should be followed in the event of boredom which is a warning sign that your spiritual side is hungry. Now, for review why do we want our spirit alive? Answer to gain the ability to talk to your soul or inner you for the best ideas or creations you can possibly make. If we are GOD as king Kanye says Let there be fun!!

## BE MINDFUL OF THE LAW OF REPEL

Now this next lesson has been blowing my mind up since its discovery in my head. Again, like clockwork after waking and remembering to open my third eye, again lessons I won't go over read another book. I turned to myself to determine what to do today. This is what was given to me. Be Mindful of the law of repel, it may or may not have been discovered yet in your reality but the law of repel is the ability to push away unwanted or un-needed energy or desire or thought. The law of Attraction brings all it can when you want something. The law of repel uses the same method but different energy. Remember the old saying I'm rubber your glue everything bounces off of me and sticks to you. I think this is where this idea came from. Think magnets ok if it helps. Mastering the law of attraction and the law of repel gives you the mental ability to truly choose what you want in life. But it uses an energy not discovered by your universe or not normally used. Dark energy or dark matter, during creation both light (good) and Dark (bad) were created to experience one another. They had to be opposites, being similar in any way means the pattern would be flawed. Creating sons, a light and a dark as their father I loved both because I am both so are you and everything else in creation. You are made in my image meaning beings of light, being as you are you naturally attract light and repel dark, look at the patterns in your head now, "WOW" Ok examples of humans attracting light are Thomas Edison, wright brothers, kids with night lights, working during the day time. We all need light to live because light is source, source is you. But for light to experience itself it must be born in darkness. Therefore, meaning all light needs dark energy to live. Light energy or light matter

consumes dark energy to create possibilities that
you choose. Now what happens to the ones you
didn't choose, well they still exist but not as a
possibility in your experience. Well depending on
the intent of that possibility it can either remain here
on lights plane. Or be moved over to the dark
energy plane where there are negative or opposite
possibilities. Since no energy dies and all thoughts
are energy and all thoughts are possible every
possibility lives. The reason you can't see them
anymore is because they have become dark. Now
we will get to the law of repel again soon. So the
energy, effort, though, and intent that goes toward
something negative is attracting dark energy in the
manner of bad or horrible possibilities for its user
and the surrounding. See dark energy and
possibilities can always be seen in plain view easily
by everyone. Why? Because being sons of light you
can always see your opposite, always see your

opponent so to speak. Sounds fair, your legal system uses right to face your accuser correct. Same thing your enemy will always be in plain sight you will always be able to physically see what your weakness or danger or villain or arch nemesis or opposite is in any set of eyes in any mental conscience state or dimensional plane ad they can do the same. Depending on perspective you will always see something you despise be it the church of god or church of Lucifer. Ok but why is that, I mean why does everything have to have an opposite? Ask yourself why do cells split and how do they divide, first movement TWO, so why does a cell divide? They divide to experience themselves. Ok kind of lame but I get it light and dark both experiencing each other through each other but both the only begotten sons of the single cell one or source. Theory of relativity, everything is connected or related you know this and so does everyone else.

After source spoke the duality began the first experience the first split light and dark the two suns Michael and Lucifer everybody sees in duels. The reason you have negative feelings is because you were born in it to become true light you must realize you are light by rejecting or repelling dark energy within you. Like a baby being born you need to clean off all the unwanted dark energy inside you. This is amazing stuff you think anyone will believe it. They can't disprove it. Ok so remember the cell again ok its first split is in half but as it becomes more complicated it becomes you. Now just because it stopped at you do you think it's finished? It isn't finished it will continue to change, evolve and grow to experience on the next level. You are not humans but simply cells experiencing themselves and humans animated by the light of the father light that created you and nurtured by mother earth. OK all the negative feelings and thoughts you conjure negative possibilities, once these are rejected after being accepted and are no longer possibilities, they become consumed by dark energy because of the lack of movement or growth they soon become easily consumed, swallowed up, eaten devoured. There is this consuming war I guess you should say going on right in front of you. Dark energy needs light to live, like nutrients; it consumes the scraps for now because it's weaker but growing. Light energy does the same it consumes dark to grow stronger. Also, just for fun Auto immune is light energy fighting light energy and cancer is light energy that refuses to share or selfish light energy. All the cells act a certain way depending on how dark energy has influenced them and just like a division in any organization or organism depending on who wins the war will depend on the survival of that unit. These two powers light and dark can also grow or attract its own to grow and build. Therefore, movement or growth is essential for life. A candle flame, dances intimidatingly in a completely dark room because it is confident in who and what it is. It knows darkness have no power over it. All light moves, it must, and all light wants to grow. Alright I can go on for ages about this but back to the law of repel. It uses dark energy or dark matter to push away unwanted energy or feelings. The law of repel uses your ability to curse something. Its dark lies or rejection of something, you see the law of attraction mastered one can consciously attract more light energy. It helps you grow when you get what you want so it's a great law for beings of light. But the law of repel is also your ability to reject what isn't wanted. Attracting is fine but what if you make a mistake does it correct itself yes if you do not reject the mistake and recreate. But to reject is one thing to curse is another both are in the law of repel.

When you are not consciously using your gifts then you are in the system or part of nature's natural pattern sometimes things happen. Being neutral in nature but our perspectives is one sided. Now when something awkward happens our conscience minds now want to meditate and ponder on it, in doing so you allow the chance to accept it or reject it or repel it. The fact that you became aware or conscience enough to think about it says something else, think noticing patterns. So, to passively reject something is no big deal, it will either be minimally consumed by dark energy if not used or remain as a possibility of acceptance later by you or someone who accepts it if it's got enough light intent to be needed or wanted by anyone. Dark energy is trash to us we don't want it but it can be useful. But if you curse it you create and entirely new possibility made purely of dark energy. It becomes strong in birth since it was born in light. It's the possibility from the

opposite of you. It seeks light energy to consume
and dark energy to attract. If the curse attaches to a
weaker being of light a sort of battle begins on the
inside. The being can still reject it but dark energy
strong like a curse is hard to defeat alone and can
diminish the power of attraction for more light help.
The dark energy is like a virus that channels more
dark energy to itself using the being of light as a
host. Once enough dark energy is gathered in the
being it becomes consumed, or as your world says
possessed with dark energy and the being entire
perspective and views and physical actions becomes
the opposite of what it truly wants... Light!  At this
point the being is sort of in an inner coma, having
full conscience of its exterior but feels out of
control or powerless to change it. Most good ideas
are changed or consumed before reaching the
exterior. The inner voice is held in captivity. To be
set free cleansing of the soul is needed. Light beings

need to recognize and help otherwise the dark energy can slowly take over your world one being at a time. To clean a being of darkness bring them to the light or enlighten them on the beauty of their world and who we are. Inspire them and help their light grow, help them rejoice and have fun, be loved and the darkness in all of you can be cast out using the law of repel.

## **GREG'S 10 COMMANDMENTS**

1. Control What you hear

2. Control What you see

3. Control how you feel

4. Pretend and live it

5. Invest in what you want

6. Nothing Can be proven, it's all perspective

7. No one else's plan can work for you, GOD speaks to individuals

8. To beat karma, apply love, Jesus defeated karma. It's just a controlled feeling

9. Nothing and no one have a fate, nothing is certain or set in stone

10. Faith is action without proof to see faith in action look for patterns or unexplained phenomena (Not Logic) faith is spirit.

## THE WISDOM OF I

There are so many days when I doubt my thoughts, so many times when I feel that if this is infinite wisdom, I am speaking to then why can't I have access to it now it's needed. Some of the things I think about would amaze you and honestly, I don't have enough time in the day to Research every thought. I mean it's impossible, I tried one day and the more I researched the more I thought about more at that moment it felt like infinite wisdom, but I didn't know How to access it all the time except through meditation or sleep. Now in the busy fast paced life of the outside world it seems that I or this wisdom inside of me moves to slow. It tells me that we as people need to slow down. What's the rush? Life is about enjoying moments not speeding through them. But for me this is unsatisfactory, I enjoy experiencing things fast and slowing down isn't happening anytime soon. It seems that this wisdom inside of me does not understand human behavior. It constantly asks me, what do you want and to that I reply everything. You have already been given everything you can possibly want can't you see it. NO! And I never feel like I have anything. After that my mind went into this deep cycle of wise sayings, quotes and inspiring concepts I wrote down as much as I could catch and remember.

1. The purpose of life is to become GOD (Mentally) I laughed when I thought that until a little more clarity came. A lot of human rulers have come to this epiphany and all have misinterpreted. To become GOD mentally is not to create a dictatorship and feel that you are better than the masses. But to open your mind to the acceptance of

whom we are inside. Life's purpose if you wish to put it that way I guess would be to go through experiences and through them learn that you are all GODS in your thoughts and actions. As it is in heaven, so it is on earth and where is heaven, not in the clouds but it's all in your mind like everything else.

2.  Remember that other people are in your life for a reason and you are not in theirs. The only opinion that matters in your world is your own. Verifying what you already feel and know only distorts what's in your head and can lead to possible futures in your reality that you are not happy with. Follow yourself.

3.  You are not punished for your sins and suffer later in "a torture chamber", you are punished BY your sins and suffer consequences NOW. Many people live by

the point system and it very popular in religions now days. They keep records and logs of what they can and cannot do while they ignore their hearts. Your actions don't count your thoughts do. Sin is violation of universal laws and Karma is its police. Just like your court systems. You do a crime now you get punished now.

4. Speak in I or I Am to create reality. Do not speak in future as it isn't now. Many people say what they will do, or are going to do. They say what they will be or want to be as if it isn't possible NOW. Nothing defines what you are but your thoughts and actions. Even if you are certified as a specific Job but mentally you relate to your hobbies when asked you will say your job is A, but you are B. example my job is a paralegal, but you are a writer.

5.  Remember your thoughts are like movie previews of future possibilities of your life. Find something good for me to watch and just press play. Many people cannot figure out what they want to be because they think they can only choose one movie. This is not true; your life isn't defined by what you are. If the movie you are watching is boring or uninteresting change it to another. Who says you can't and who is going to stop you.

6.  Take inventory of you, skills talents like's dislikes accomplishments goals and failures. You must know who you are and what you bring to this world naturally. In finding this you can discover your true path of what you want. But remember even if you find this you still have a choice. You can say, Hey I'm supposed to be a teacher in life, but at the same time say. I would like to try being

a nurse first. Your inventory will point to something big and if you can't find your way check your supplies it could give a clue.

7.  Protect and build your family and future generations. Remember this is a future YOU. As you are a parent to your children your children will surely become a parent to you. Many people believe in a second or multiple lives, so this concept isn't new. They think they will come back as anything not true you come back as a future generation of yourself. Your ancestors are yourself you already know your history you made it. Protect family secrets

8.  Always invest in more than you fear you can. This builds your future with knowledge and insight. You should go hard in your experiences you are the only person that can benefit from what you do. So, do it right and

do it how you feel you should. It instantly
becomes your history.

9.  You do not have to repeat prior experiences.
    Most people even if they live a short life can
    experience almost everything your world
    has to offer and in doing so you will grow
    wiser and be happier. The fact that people
    contain themselves in a protective shell
    repeating the same experiences day after day
    is very surprising. I still don't understand
    what's so fun about what you already know.

10. Make your best attempt at everything you
    do. Do not get caught in the illusion of time
    it's not real. Time can be overcome simply
    by ignoring it. How many times to try
    something count more against you than the
    time spent doing it? Remember it's not what
    you are that holds you back but what you

THINK you are. Because you are what you think you are.

## "VIRTUES OF LIFE"

1) *Acceptance:* Embracing life on its own terms. Acceptance allows us to bend without breaking in the face of tests. To consider circumstances, especially those that cannot be changed, as satisfactory.

2) *Accountability:* The willingness to take full responsibility for our choices.

3) *Appreciation:* Seeing the good in life. Freely expressing gratitude.

4) *Assertiveness:* Telling the truth about what is just, setting clear boundaries.

5) *Awe:* Reverence and wonder, deep respect for the source of life.

6) *Beauty:* A sense of wonder and reverence for the harmony, color, and loveliness of the world. Calling on our creativity to add to the beauty in the world.

7) *Bravery:* A quality of spirit that enables you to face danger of pain without showing fear. caring

8) *Caring:* Giving tender attention to the people and things that matter to us. Listening with compassion, helping with kindness.

9) *Caution:* Avoidance of rashness, attention to safety.

10) *Charity:* A giving heart, a generous way of viewing others and caring for their needs.

11) *Cheerfulness:* Seeing the bright side, looking for the good in whatever happens.

12) *Cleanliness:* Keeping our bodies, our thoughts and our spaces clean. An environment of order and beauty brings peace to our souls.

13) *Commitment:* Caring deeply about a person, a goal or a belief. Willingness to give our all and keep our promises.

14) *Compassion:* Deep empathy for the suffering of others. Compassion flows freely from the heart when we let go of judgments and seek to understand.

15) *Confidence:* A sense of assurance that comes from having faith in ourselves and in life. Confidence allows us to trust that we have the strength to cope with whatever happens.

16) *Consideration:* Giving careful thought to the needs of others. Holding a decision in a contemplative and thoughtful way.

17) *Contentment:* The awareness of sufficiency, a sense that we have enough, and we are enough. Appreciating the simple gifts of life.

18) **Cooperation:** Working together for a common goal, calling on the different gifts each of us has to offer.

19) **Courage:** Transforms fear into determination. Embracing life fully, without holding back, doing what must be done even when it is difficult or risky.

20) **Courtesy:** Treating others with kindness, tact and graciousness.

21) **Creativity:** The power of imagination. Being open to inspiration, this ignites our originality.

22) **Curiosity:** A desire to find out and know things.

23) **Decisiveness:** Firmness of mind in taking a stand, reaching a conclusion, making a decision. It requires both courage and discernment.

24) **Defiance:** Bold resistance.

25) **Detachment:** Experiencing our feelings without allowing them to control us. Stepping back and thoughtfully choosing how we will act rather than just reacting.

26) **Determination:** Firmness of purpose.

27) **Devotion:** Commitment to something we care about deeply. Wholehearted service to our life's purpose. A great love or loyalty, enthusiastic zeal.

28) *Dignity:* Honoring the worth of all people, including ourselves and treating everyone with respect.

29) *Diligence:* Doing what needs to be done with care, concentration and single-pointed attention, giving our absolute best.

30) *Discernment:* Applying the wisdom of our intuition to discover what is essential and true, with contemplative vigilance. Clarity of the soul.

31) *Discretion:* Being discrete in one's speech, keeping secrets.

32) *Endurance:* Practicing perseverance and patience when obstacles arise hones our character and educates our souls. We welcome all that we are here to learn.

33) *Enthusiasm:* Being filled with spirit. Excitement about life and openness to the wonders each day holds. Acting wholeheartedly, with zeal and eagerness, holding nothing back.

34) *Excellence:* Giving our best to any task we do and any relationship we have.

35) *Fairness:* Seeking justice, giving each person their share, making sure that everyone's needs are met.

36) *Faith:* A relationship of trust. Belief in the reality of Grace.

37) **Faithfulness:** Loyalty to our beliefs, regardless of what happens. Being true to the people we love.

38) **Fidelity:** Abiding by an agreement, treating it as a sacred covenant. Complete faithfulness in our relationships.

39) **Flexibility:** The ability to adapt and change amid the fluctuating circumstances of life. Going with the flow. Adaptable, able to be changed to suit circumstances.

40) **Focus:** Concentrated awareness and effort.

41) **Forbearance:** Tolerating hardship with good grace. Not allowing the trials of life to steal our joy.

42) **Forgiveness:** Overlooking mistakes and being willing to move forward with a clean slate. Forgiving others frees us from resentment. Forgiving ourselves is part of positive change. To cease to feel angry or bitter towards a person or about an offence.

43) **Fortitude:** Strength of character. The will to endure no matter what happens, with courage and patience.

44) **Friendliness:** A spiritual essential. Reaching out to others with warmth and caring. The willingness to be an intimate companion.

45) **Generosity:** Giving fully, sharing freely. Trust that there is plenty for everyone. Giving or ready to give freely, free from meanness or prejudice.

46) *Gentleness:* Moving wisely, touching softly, speaking quietly and thinking kindly. Moderate; mild, quite; not rough or severe.

47) *Grace:* Openness to the bounties of life, trusting that we are held in God's love through all circumstances. Reflecting gentleness and beauty in the way we act, speak and move.

48) *Gratitude:* Freely expressing thankfulness and appreciation to others and for the gifts of life.

49) *Gratitude:* Being thankful.

50) *Helpfulness:* Doing useful things that make a difference to others. Taking time for thoughtfulness.

51) *Honesty:* Being truthful, sincere, open, and genuine. The confidence to be ourselves. Sincere; not lying or cheating.

52) *Honor:* Living with a sense of respect for what we know is right. Living up to the virtues of our character. Keeping our agreements with integrity.

53) *Hope:* Looking to the future with trust and faith. Optimism in the face of adversity.

54) *Humanity:* Having an attitude of caring and mercy to all people.

55) *Humbleness:* Modest; not arrogant or boastful.

56) **Humility:** Being open to every lesson life brings, trusting that our mistakes are often our best teachers. Being thankful for our gifts instead of boastful.

57) **Humor:** The ability to perceive, enjoy, or express what is amusing, comical, incongruous, or absurd.

58) **Idealism:** Caring about what is right and meaningful in life. Daring to have big dreams and then acting as if they are possible.

59) **Impartiality:** Fair.

60) **Independence:** Self-reliance. Making our own choices confidently without undue influence from others. Perceiving the truth, with trust in our own discernment.

61) **Industry:** Diligent, hardworking.

62) **Initiative:** Daring to be original. Using our creativity to bring something new into the world.

63) **Innocence:** Guileless, not guilty.

64) **Integrity:** Standing on moral high ground. Keeping faith with our ideals and our agreements.

65) **Joyfulness:** An inner wellspring of peace and happiness. Enjoying the richness of life. Finding humor, even in the midst of hard times.

66) *Justice:* Being fair in all we do. Making amends when we have hurt or wronged others. Protecting everyone's rights, including our own. Fair, impartial, giving a deserved response.

67) *Kindness:* Showing compassion. Giving tender attention in ways that brings others happiness. Friendly, helpful, well meaning.

68) *Love:* The connection between one heart and another. Attraction, affection and caring for a person, a place, an idea, and for life itself. A deep, tender, ineffable feeling of affection and solicitude toward a person, such as that arising from kinship, recognition of attractive qualities, or a sense of underlying oneness.

69) *Loyalty:* Unwavering faithfulness and commitment to people and ideas we care about, through good times and bad. Steadfast in allegiance to one's homeland, government, or sovereign. Faithful to a person, ideal, custom, cause, or duty.

70) *Majesty:* Great and impressive dignity.

71) *Mercy:* Blessing others with our compassion and forgiveness. Extending our tenderness beyond what is just or deserved.

72) *Mindfulness:* Living reflectively and meaningfully, with conscious awareness of our actions, our words and our thoughts.

73) *Moderation:* Being content with enough. Using self-discipline to create balance in our lives and to keep from overdoing. Healthy stewardship of our time and resources. The avoidance of extremes in one's actions or opinions.

74) *Modesty:* Self-respect and quiet confidence. Accepting praise with humility and gratitude. A sense of respectful privacy about our bodies.

75) *Nobility:* Having high moral standards. Doing the right thing. Keeping faith with our true value as spiritual beings.

76) *Obedience:* Following what we know is right. Compliance with the law. Abiding by our deepest integrity and conquering our misplaced passions. Willingness to obey, to be controlled when necessary, to carry out orders.

77) *Openness:* Willingness to consider new ideas. Listening to others with humility and sincerity. Being receptive to the blessings and surprises of life. Openness: Ready and willing to talk candidly. Non-secretive.

78) *Orderliness:* Creating an environment of peace and order. Planning step by step instead of going in circles.

79) *Patience:* Waiting peacefully. Quiet hope and faith that things will turn out right. The ability to endure delay, trouble, pain or hardship.

80) *Peacefulness:* Inner calm and tranquility. Giving up the love of power for the power of love. Resolving conflict in a just and gentle way. Freedom from mental agitation; serenity.

81) *Perceptiveness:* Clarity of insight. Understanding that is intuitive, discerning and accurate.

82) *Perseverance:* Staying the course for however long it takes. Steadfastness and persistence in pursuing our goals.

83) *Prayerfulness:* A relationship of faith and gratitude with a power and presence greater than ourselves. A conversation with God.

84) *Prudence:* Wise or careful in conduct. Shrewd or thrifty in planning ahead.

85) *Purity:* A process of freeing ourselves day by day from influences and attachments that keep us from being true to ourselves and to what we know is right. Physical and spiritual cleanliness.

86) *Purposefulness:* Awareness of the meaningfulness of our lives. Living by a clear vision and focusing our energy on the goal before us.

87) *Reliability:* Being dependable. Being a promise keeper. Taking responsibility with trustworthiness. Can be trusted to do something.

88) **Respect:** An attitude of honoring oneself and others through our words and actions. Treating every person with dignity and courtesy.

89) **Responsibility:** The willingness to be accountable for our choices and also for our mistakes. Taking on what is ours to do with strength and reliability. Having control over and accountability for appropriate events.

90) **Reverence:** An awareness of the sacredness of life. Living with wonder and faith. Having a routine of reflection.

91) **Righteousness:** Living by a code of spiritual rectitude. Impeccable integrity to what we know is right. Calling ourselves gently back when we go off track.

92) **Sacrifice:** The willingness to give up what is important to us for what we know is more important. Giving our all for our beliefs. Making our life a sacred offering.

93) **Self-Discipline:** The self-control to do only what we truly choose to do, without being blown off course by our desires. Establishing healthy and ennobling habits.

94) **Sensitivity:** Heightened awareness of oneself and others within the context of social and personal relationships.

95) **Serenity:** Tranquility of spirit, with trust and faith that all will be well. Peacefulness in the midst of trials.

96) **Service:** Doing helpful things that make a difference to others. Investing excellence in everything we do. The contribution we make is the fruitage of our lives.

97) **Simplicity:** Straightforward; not complex or complicated. Unpretentious.

98) **Sincerity:** Being open and genuine. Our words and actions reflect a truthful heart. Free from pretense or deceit in manner or actions.

99) **Sobriety:** Serious, solemn and calm. Free from intoxication.

100) **Spontaneity:** Natural, not planned.

101) **Steadfastness:** Being steady, persevering and dependable. Having the strength to remain true to our purpose in spite of obstacles that arise.

102) **Steadfastness:** Firm, resolute; determinedly unwavering.

103) **Strength:** The inner power to withstand whatever comes. Endurance in the midst of tests. Capable of exerting great force.

104) **Tact:** Telling the truth kindly. Thinking before we speak, aware of how deeply our words affect others. Discerning what to say, when it is timely to say it, and what is better left unsaid.

105)    *Temperance:* Moderation in our speech and our appetites. Using self-restraint in the midst of temptation.

106)    *Thankfulness:* An attitude of gratitude for living, learning, loving and being. Generosity in expressing appreciation. Focusing on the blessings in our lives.

107)    *Tolerance:* Being open to differences. Refraining from judgments. Patience and forgiveness with others and ourselves. Accepting things that we wish were different with humor and grace.

108)    *Toughness:* Strong and durable; not easily damaged.

109)    *Tranquility:* Serenely quiet and peaceful; undisturbed.

110)    *Trust:* Having faith. Positive expectation that all will be well. Having confidence that the right thing will come about without trying to control it or make it happen. Being sure, in the depths of our being, that there is some gift or learning in everything that happens. Having confidence in others; lacking suspicion.

111)    *Trustworthiness:* Being worthy of the trust others place in us. When we give our word, we stand by it. Keeping our agreements faithfully. Able to be trusted or depended on; reliable.

112)    *Truthfulness:* Truth is the bedrock of integrity on which we build all our other virtues. An ongoing

commitment to live by what is most real and authentic in our own nature. Honesty in all our dealings.

113) **_Understanding:_** Being insightful in our perceptions of ideas and feelings. Listening with compassion and accuracy to others' feelings.

114) **_Unity:_** Inclusiveness. Finding common ground in our diversity. Seeking peace in all circumstances.

115) **_Uprightness:_** Following what is right and moral. Standing up for honesty and justice. Living in integrity.

116) **_Wisdom:_** Having a discerning mind based on experience and mindfulness. Making wise decisions based on our deepest intuition.

117) **_Zeal:_** Fervent enthusiasm for what we believe to be important, Living by a strong sense of the value of life and faith.

www.ingramcontent.com/pod-product-compliance
Lightning Source LLC
Chambersburg PA
CBHW070032100426
42740CB00013B/2671